GOD'S ORIGINAL DESIGN

A BLUEPRINT FOR LIFE ON EARTH

ABRAHAM JOHN

God's Original Design: A Blueprint for Life on Earth
DISCIPLING NATIONS SERIES # 3

Copyright © 2020 by Abraham John

Published by Abraham John

www.TheKingdomNetwork.org
email: info@thekingdomnetwork.org
1-800-558-5020

ISBN: 978-1-948330-08-4

Printed in the United States of America

Unless otherwise indicated, all Scriptures are from the New King James Version®. Copyright © 1982 by Thomas Nelson. Used by permission.

Scripture quotations marked (NLT) are taken from the Holy Bible, New Living Translation, copyright © 1996, 2004, 2015 by Tyndale House Foundation. Used by permission of Tyndale House Publishers, Inc., Carol Stream, Illinois 60188. All rights reserved.

Scripture quotations marked (KJV) are from the King James Version and are in the public domain.

All *emphases* or additions in parentheses within scriptural quotations are the author's own.

All rights reserved. No part of this book may be reproduced or transmitted in any form or by any means, electronic or mechanical, including photocopying, recording, or by any information storage and retrieval system, without permission in writing from the author. Please direct your inquiries to info@thekingdomnetwork.org.

CONTENTS

Preface	5
Introduction	9
Chapter 1: The Shift—*Change Is Here*, Part I	13
Chapter 2: The Shift—*Change is Here*, Part II	35
Chapter 3: God's Original Blueprint	61
Chapter 4: God's Seven Eternal Purposes, Part I	69
Chapter 5: God's Seven Eternal Purposes, Part II	85
Chapter 6: The Third Temple	99
Chapter 7: The Original Design	111
Chapter 8 The Power of Kingdom Purpose	133
Chapter 9: The Power of Kingdom Identity	157
Chapter 10: Three Layers of Revelation Hidden in the Parable	179
Chapter 11: The Power of Kingcom Birthright	189
Chapter 12: The Process of Receiving the Fatted Calf	205
Chapter 13: Manifestation of the Sons of God	217
Chapter 14: Leadership vs. Sonship	231
Chapter 15: Ten Stages of Discipleship	243
Chapter 16: Three Kinds of People We Need to Fulfill Our Kingdom Assignment	261
More Books & Resources	269

PREFACE

When something goes wrong with a product or a structure, it is normal for engineers to look to the blueprint used to manufacture or build it. To diagnose a problem that causes malfunctioning, blueprints are essential.

If you look at life and the state of our planet, you will quickly realize that life on earth is not going as it was intended. Almost everything is malfunctioning or at some level of dysfunction. We have been blaming sin, the devil, global warming, end times, and corrupt politicians for all the chaos around us for too long.

Jesus came to solve the problems that were caused by sin and the devil. But we have limited the outcome of what Jesus did to just barely making it to heaven after we die. Once we were saved, we didn't take time to look at God's blueprint for life and the earth.

Only when we understand the blueprint will we be able to compare where we are to where we are supposed to be—or where we could be. In order to rightly diagnose the problem and come up with a solution, we need to look at the original blueprint.

When you go to a doctor with your symptoms, the reason they are able to prescribe treatment is because they will make a diagnosis to understand which part of the body is malfunctioning and why. Then they compare that part of the body to the knowledge they have about how it is supposed to function when your body is healthy.

They spend years studying the human body to be able to diagnose diseases correctly. Only when they compare the symptoms with a healthy body are they are able to treat it properly. Treatments are intended to bring the body back to its original state and function.

They go to microscopic levels, sometimes even to the DNA, to correctly comprehend our bodies and how they function. But before they study sickness and disease, it is important to study a healthy body and how all parts are *supposed* to function.

That is what we should have done in the body of Christ. When we noticed something in life or on earth was not functioning properly, we should have gone and looked at the blueprint before we drew a conclusion. Before we misjudge and conclude the death and destruction of the earth, we need to spend time looking at how it all began and the reason why it is in the state it is today.

Comparing against the Blueprint

If Jesus solved the sin problem and the devil problem, then why is life not functioning the way it is supposed to? When we find the answer to that question, then we will understand how our world has been falling apart to the point is has today.

If a medical practitioner prescribes treatment before he or she gives a proper diagnosis and without understanding the human body, they will lose their license to practice medicine. They could even go to prison! We have to ask ourselves: How much time have we spent studying the original plan and purpose of God for the earth and mankind compared to how much we study end-time predictions and assumptions? Very little; we assume we know all about it and all along we messed it up, refusing to take any responsibility for the damage we caused.

We are so caught up with the idea of flying away from the earth that we parrot songs about it without even thinking where the songs came from. Some may say that they sing those songs because that is what their grandparents sang. But that is what parrots and monkeys do—they do the same things their ancestors did. They do not have the mental faculties to stop and think about why they are doing what they are doing. Humans are not created to be like that.

Once we are saved from our sins, it is our responsibility to go back and look at the blueprint to find out how life should have been on the earth if there was no sin—if Adam did not fall. Then we should compare it with how life is now, do a diagnosis, and come up with a proper *treatment plan* to restore it to match the blueprint. That is the real assignment of a born-again believer.

In order to treat and solve any problem we face in our world today, it is important to compare the current world system and the condition of the earth with God's original blueprint. After reading this book you will have a glimpse of how life should have been and how God intended for life to function from the beginning.

That is the purpose of this book. You will have an *idea* of how life should have been on this planet and what was in God's heart and mind when He designed Earth and our lives. After you study this book, I would encourage you to compare it with your life and identify the areas that are not working according to God's design and come up with a proper treatment plan to bring them back into alignment with the blueprint.

That should be the purpose of all Christian education, every discipleship program, and seminary. If you do not know where to go to find the proper training, I encourage you to join one of our Kingdom Schools in different parts of the earth. Please see the last page for more information.

Once you have brought your life back into alignment with the blueprint, I encourage you not to stop there. Look around and identify at least one area where you can contribute with the gifts and potential God has deposited in you and bring it back into alignment to the original plan. That is your calling. Welcome to the journey!

INTRODUCTION

When the COVID-19 pandemic happened, people around the world began to wonder if this was the end of the world. As usual, when something tragic happens, Christians around the world began to assume that the rapture was going to take place any minute. But this was not the end of the world, but it *was* the end of things as we knew it. This was not the end of the church age either but the end of the church as we knew it.

The Lord is recalibrating and realigning His church, along with the entire world system and our planet. Some are calling it a global reset. It is imperative for us to understand the importance of the times. We are living in a significant moment in history.

What if what we were taught about life and church were not completely true? We were taught that we need to go to school, and then college, and then find a good job or start a business. Making money and living a good life is all there is. What if that wasn't true and there was a better reason for our lives on earth?

We were taught that our purpose is to glorify God or to live for the glory of God. This meant that we should live life like everybody else, work hard, make some money, and be good Christians by going to church, giving tithes, and witnessing for Jesus whenever we could. But what if there was a better way to impact more lives and bring more souls into the kingdom without ever *preaching* a single sermon?

Mankind has been on a detour for thousands of years. Because we have gone so far in the wrong direction for so long, nobody realizes where it all began or how we got where we are now. The majority of us live the way we do because that is what everybody else around us is doing.

Very few people dare to stop, think, and ask for directions to get back on the right track. They are asking: Why are we doing what we are doing? What if what we thought was normal was never supposed to be normal? What if everything that we were taught by the church and others was not true?

This book is written to that particular group of people who are willing to stop and ask questions about how we got here—to those who are feeling dissatisfaction and discontentment with what is going on in their lives. They are asking, "Is there a way out of this mundane thing we call life? Why is family life not working? Why don't people care about life anymore? Why we are afraid to speak the truth?" The majority are weary and tired; they just don't know what to do.

What if what you thought about church wasn't completely true, either? Many are afraid, believing that if they do not "go to" church on a Sunday morning, God will be displeased or punish them. Because of the pandemic, church buildings all around the world were closed and we haven't heard any news about God striking anyone dead with lightning because they didn't go to church on a Sunday!

I believe God allowed the pandemic to happen in order to shut the doors of all the religious centers for a few months. In order to let Christians know that what He thinks about church and what we have been doing for many years are two different things.

We thought church was someplace we go to on a Sunday morning to do some religious rituals to make God happy so that nothing will go wrong for the next six days. Many went to church out of fear—fear of being punished by God if they didn't go. Others went to hear a sermon, and some others went to socialize with their friends.

What if you have been exploited and taken advantage of by the religious system and the spirit that is working behind it? They may have promised some material blessings using utopian ideologies that haven't worked either for the people who promised them or for you all these years. Then finally, the religious system promised us an entry ticket to heaven after we die.

This book is written to that particular group of people who are tired of religion and church as usual. I hope and pray that you will find your way back into your original blueprint and assignment in the kingdom of our Father.

What if the salvation we received and taught were incomplete? Salvation came because of the fall of Adam. But most people are unaware from where Adam fell and what he lost when he fell. Nobody in the Bible offered salvation as a ticket to go to heaven. In fact, nobody in the Bible ever asked anyone if they want to go to heaven when they die. Not even Jesus!

Jesus never said He is the way to heaven. That is what most people have believed and preached. He said that He is the way to the Father. Humans are looking for a Father that they lost—not heaven. They lost sonship. I have not yet met a single human being who wished he or she could die and leave this planet when they are having a good day. We all have wished to leave this planet when things were hard and when life wasn't easy.

Then the question is: How did we get here? The more important question is: How do we get back on the right track from where we took the detour? Is it even possible now?

If we do not discover God's original design for our lives and the church, ladies and gentlemen, I want to tell you that there's no hope for our future or for humanity. Please realize that I am not saying this lightly. We are already late, and time is running out. We should have done this fifty or even five hundred years ago. But as the old saying goes, it's better late than never.

If we do not take a stand now, it will be too late. The enemy is already scheming to destroy millions of lives before they ever get a chance to understand life and discover God's unique plan for their lives.

This book is written to those who are asking questions in their hearts about life, church, heaven, death, rapture, and the purpose for which they were sent here, but cannot find any satisfying answers. I hope and pray that you will find the answers in this book.

Welcome to the journey of discovering God's original design and plan for your life and for planet Earth. If you read something that you do not understand, please ask the Holy Spirit to open your eyes and give you understanding, as well as the courage to make the necessary change in your life. Once you discover the truth and freedom it brings, don't keep it for yourself. Share it with your friends and family so that they can benefit from it. Thank you!

CHAPTER 1

THE SHIFT—*CHANGE IS HERE*, PART I

At the end of each year, I ask the Lord to give me a word for the coming year. What He gave me for 2020 was three words: *change*, *fulfillment*, and *kingdom*. Then He said, "Get ready for change; you will have to learn new ways of doing things in every aspect of your life."

The Lord told me that this change would affect mainly three areas of our lives: family and social relationships, our relationship with God (religion and church), and the economy of the world. We have seen all of these unfolding in 2020. The world we knew changed and it will never be the same again. Relationships, the economy, the travel industry, educational systems, church, and everything else has changed.

If we do not adapt to the change that is taking place, we will miss the next season. These changes are not just taking place in external circumstances; they are happening inside of us. We are not the same people we were last year. Things have shifted in our spirit man since this pandemic started.

2020 was also a year of fulfillment. For many, things they have been waiting for God to do in their lives for years were fulfilled this year. There will be an acceleration of fulfillment concerning things that pertain to your personal assignment in the kingdom.

Many new doors that are related to your destiny will be opened. Things and people will come into alignment so that you can go into the next level of your calling. Missing pieces will finally come together and make sense of everything you've been through.

I personally know people who could not find a mate for more than fifty years who got engaged in 2020. Many of our ministry partners have had the best year in their businesses. One businessman told me that July 2020 was the best month of his entire business history. New assignments were birthed for many. Many people have been launched into their kingdom assignment. Some others moved to new locations to fulfill their kingdom assignment.

There are more people talking and preaching about the kingdom of God than any other year—and from now on it will continue to increase year by year, until the gospel of the kingdom is preached in all the world and in every nation as a witness.

Transition Is Coming

The word the Lord gave me for 2021 is that it will be a year of transition into the kingdom. From this year onward, we are beginning that process of transition. The earth and all creation are going through birth pangs; they cannot wait to be free from the bondage of corruption. This will continue over the next few years.

There are four foundational areas where this transition will be happening:

1. From religion to the kingdom
2. From church to *ekklesia*
3. From Old Covenant rituals to New Covenant realities
4. From being employed to walking in our kingdom assignment

These are not the only areas where transition is taking place, but they are the foundational ones.

Over the next few chapters I will explain in detail about these four main areas of transition. The sooner you make those transitions, the sooner you will be in alignment with God to fulfill your assignment in the kingdom.

As people walk into transition, more will start preaching the gospel of the kingdom all over the world. Many believers will come to understand what the kingdom of God is all about and will find their places in it. They will wake up to their eternal kingdom assignment.

Personally, though it's been an emotionally intense year, this pandemic has been the best thing that has ever happened for us as a ministry. During this locked-down period, God has birthed the Kingdom School, and hundreds of students from across the globe have gone through the training. It is exciting to see them being released into fulfilling their kingdom assignment as the result of the training they received.

We reached more people in more nations with the gospel of the kingdom during the lockdown than any other time before. Thank God for technology and the Internet! People from more than fifty countries visited our website. More people ordered books from our website than during any of the previous years. All glory belongs to God!

Crisis Brings Kingdom Opportunity

God has His way of working out His purpose through and during floods, famines, wars, and crises. He is an expert in navigating His children through these natural calamities to see His plan come to fulfillment in their lives and in their countries. There is a kingdom opportunity hidden in every natural crisis, but most people do not recognize it.

Every time a crisis arises in the natural, it is an opportune time for God's kingdom citizens to be promoted. However, we have been so programmed with a doom-and-gloom theology that when the crisis appears, the church begins to sing their end-time songs. They miss out on what God has for them and they remain the same, or their situation goes from bad to worse.

This will only change when we understand God's original design and purpose, and then bring our lives into alignment to that design. But this will not happen automatically just because we are good Christians or go to church on a Sunday morning.

Heaven is never in panic mode, and the kingdom of God is not under lockdown. Kingdom economy never goes through recession or inflation. His kingdom is an everlasting kingdom, and His dominion endures throughout all generations.

The Bible says there is a time coming when God will shake everything so that what cannot be shaken might remain (Hebrews 12:27). There is only one thing that cannot be shaken—His kingdom. But before God shakes everything, He wants His children to be prepared and be sure they are protected and taken care of. That is the reason He gave me this book and the Kingdom School. Sooner or later, He will shake everything. The question is: Are you prepared?

The Kingdom Should Have the Answers

While I am writing this, the whole world is under the threat of a virus. Thousands of lives are being lost and millions are affected by it. Nations and cities are under lockdown. In many places, people have been forced to stay home for months. Many schools and colleges are closed. Streets are empty and shops have remained closed for months. Businesses and travel industries have been affected immensely. People are uncertain about the future. It is impossible to estimate the amount of loss that the worldwide economy has suffered.

How are God's people supposed to respond to a situation like this? How do we prepare the body of Christ for something like this? Let's learn our lessons from incidents like this and prepare better for the next emergency.

During a time of emergency, God's people are the ones who are supposed to have solutions and answers. We are not supposed to act scared or anxious because our God is on the throne. We are supposed present ourselves like the Psalmist says in Psalm 46:2–3:

> Therefore we will not fear, even though the earth be removed, and though the mountains be carried into the midst of the sea; though its waters roar and be troubled, though the mountains shake with its swelling.

The Bible says God called for a famine in Egypt to promote His son Joseph (Psalm 105:16). God gave the solution to His son Joseph to prepare for the famine. He implemented a massive system for the following seven years to collect the grain in storehouses to prepare for the famine that God said would be coming over the next seven years after that—and it did not affect God's children negatively. God sent Joseph to Egypt way ahead of time to prepare food for His people, so that their lives could be spared.

Kingdom economy thrives during crises, famine, pandemics, and other disasters. That is how you know which economy you live and operate in—when you discover whether you are prospering or downsizing during these challenging times.

God used that famine in Egypt to promote and bless His people. That is the way it should happen in every crisis situation. Every time a calamity hits, God's people must rise to the top and not go into hiding. We should consider it as a time of promotion not a time of lack or to be frightened. When darkness comes upon the people of the land, light should shine on us. How do we do that in a practical way?

When God sent plagues upon Egypt, it was because it was time for the deliverance of God's people. When darkness comes upon the people of the land, know that God's light and glory is about to shine brighter upon His people. The time for the deliverance of God's people from Egypt and the Babylonian system has come. This pandemic was a clarion call for God's people all over the world to prepare for the great exodus that is ahead of us.

To navigate the change that is affecting the world negatively, and for the promotion and benefit of the body of Christ, we need to make certain shifts right now. What we have experienced so far is nothing compared to what is coming. Following are the steps or shifts we need to make to prepare ourselves for what is coming on the earth and to not be affected by it.

Shifting from Religion to the Kingdom

During the pandemic, all religious centers were closed down. Unfortunately, churches were closed down as well. Church should never have been part of any religion. Jesus is not the founder of a religion called "Christianity."

We were not created for any religion. We were created for a kingdom. We belong to the kingdom of God, and we were sent to this earth to fulfill a specific assignment for the King of the kingdom. Religion will never satisfy us. Religion will only put us in perpetual misery by telling us to keep on doing the same things we always did and expecting a different result.

For too long, the kingdom of God has been hijacked and misrepresented by a religion called "Christianity," with all of its different versions and denominations. Below are the some of the dangers of following a religion.

DANGERS OF RELIGION

Religion makes us something we were never meant to be

Religion will take a human who is created in the image and likeness of God and make a person of mere habits and rituals. We were created to function like God functions.

Religion limits our potential

If you plant an oak tree in a pot and keep it inside a house, that tree will never grow to its full size, even though it has the potential. That is what religion will do to us. God created us with enormous potential.

Religion puts us in a cage or a box

If you take a shark and put it in a glass container, that shark will not grow beyond the size of that container. The shark has the potential to grow several feet long and some can weigh thousands of pounds. That is why a religious church system can never produce or raise up people like Elon Musk, Steve Jobs, or Bill Gates. We were created to live in a kingdom.

Religion limits vision

Religion thrives in pipe dreams. It constricts and twists the truth, stealing or limiting our vision. Religion limits God. It takes a God who is unlimited in every way and puts Him inside a building that is made by hands.

Religion kills creativity

Our God is the most creative Person in the universe. Holy Spirit is the architect of the universe. I grew up in a denomination that gloried in wearing white clothes. They taught me every other color is demonic and that if you want to be really holy, you had to wear white clothing. If you wore a different color, you were considered backslidden. The religious spirit is that ridiculous!

Religion makes us unproductive

Religious people are the most unproductive group of people on planet Earth. There is nothing good about religion. If you look at people that are religious, their productivity will be so low. There are two groups of people on the earth: producers and consumers. Church became the most consuming agency on the earth.

Religion is all about conditioning

The purpose of religion is to condition our brains in a certain way so that we will not think or function outside of it. They have done this study on animals. If you ring a bell every time you feed a dog, after a while, every time that dog hears that bell, it will think it is time to eat. That is what brain- or mind-conditioning means.

When you become religious, you automatically behave and think a certain way. For example, when a religious person hears a particular style or beat of music, suddenly he or she will begin to clap or show some specific mannerisms. That is the religious spirit working and not the unique, creative ways of God. It will take years to correct and heal the brain damage religion has caused in people.

Religion thrives on wishful thinking and unattainable promises and goals

Every religion has some common traits. They all promise the "pie-in-the-sky" unrealistic goals. It says that someday, things will get better and that the past was so great but there is nothing for the present. People die in their wishful thinking without ever seeing or experiencing fulfillment. Instead of fulfilling their calling, they just wait around, wishing for things to change.

Religion will kill you before you discover or fulfill your purpose

That is a fact. One preacher said the cemetery is the wealthiest place on the planet because it holds all the dreams that were never fulfilled, businesses that were never started, songs that were never sung, and books that were never written. Inventions and ideas that could have changed the world have been buried with people in their graves.

The religious system will not only squash your vision and dreams, but it will hold them underwater and drown them out before they can ever be actualized. This is why it is so crucial for people to transition out of religion, so they can actually walk into what God called them to do.

Religion takes a unique individual and creates a puppet or a copy out of them

Religion is all about programs and rituals, which is the polar opposite of the way God is. God is creative and original. Think of all the creatures on earth and in the ocean—they are all different from each other, and all of them fulfill special and unique places in the natural world. God created each person the same way; we are all unique individuals with specific missions to accomplish for the kingdom.

Religion comes along and tells us all that we have to look a certain way, do the same things as each other, and that if anyone steps out of those preconceived, boxed-in programs and rituals, then you don't fit. The goal is to turn you into a puppet to do and say whatever they want you to do and say instead of walking in your unique calling.

Religion creates alternative and fake realities

I have seen some things that are common in all religions. If people can reach a certain emotional state or a frenzied feeling, then they think they have attained a certain level of spirituality. In Christianity, they call this the anointing. How sad! This is not the anointing—the anointing was given to accomplish a certain task, and that is not possible in our own strength. It is not given to make us feel good.

Religion causes you to serve the devil and then say you are serving God

Another sad thing that religion does is deceive people into believing that they are serving God when they are really serving the devil and his kingdom! How is this possible? It does it by shifting our focus to the very opposite of what God is trying to accomplish.

This happened to the Jewish religious leaders during Jesus' time. They thought they were serving God. In truth, they were serving the devil with their whole hearts but couldn't recognize it because of deception.

I was in that state for a long time. I thought I was serving God, but I was fighting against the very purpose of God by trying to take people out of this planet. While God is trying to see His kingdom come to earth, I was trying to vacate earth.

Religion Is a Poison That Slowly Kills People Without Their Knowledge

You might have heard the phrase *frog in a kettle*. If you put a frog into hot water suddenly, it will not stay there. It will realize the danger and jump right out immediately. But, if you heat up the frog in a kettle, it will never jump out of the kettle because the water warms so gradually that it doesn't even notice that it is being killed.

That is what religion does to people. It will slowly drain our creativity, steal our purpose, vision, and productivity, and at the end we will just wait to die. Please don't let that happen to you!

Tired of Religion

People everywhere are tired of the church and religion as usual. Because of the hypocrisy they saw in churches and religion, many people went the opposite direction and became extreme liberals. They were tired of all the dos and don'ts of religion. The solution to religion is not liberalism, but the kingdom. Sadly, no one has presented the kingdom to these people.

We have a whole new generation of people in America and Europe who are liberals. They don't want to do anything with God or the church. Most of them grew up in religious background or families. We failed to give them the kingdom of God, so the enemy came in and stole their souls.

They are searching and longing for something, but they are not sure what that is yet. In truth, their hearts are longing for the lost kingdom. They don't know that until they hear the gospel of the kingdom. The moment they hear it, their spirits will resonate to the message.

Many have closed their hearts to God and religion because of this misrepresentation. It will take a miracle to turn their hearts and opinions around to the kingdom. May the Lord help us do that.

RELIGION VERSUS THE KINGDOM

Here are some of the differences between religion and the kingdom:

Religion tries to please God by being good and doing good works

There are many people out there who think they are good people and are convinced that they do not need any God in their lives.

In the kingdom, God is already pleased with us and nothing we could ever do will cause Him to accept us or love us more. He accepted us in the beloved and made us holy and blameless before the foundation of the world (Ephesians 1:4). He knew us before we were born in our mother's womb (Jeremiah 1:5). He sent us to this planet for a specific assignment (Ephesians 2:10).

People like Jeremiah and John the Baptist in the Bible are the best examples of this. What they did or did not do while growing up had nothing to do with what they were called to do—it was predetermined by God before they arrived on this planet.

The kingdom is about announcing the acceptable year of the Lord

Since the coming of Jesus, a new era began, an era every Old Testament saint looked forward to. They were all tired of trying to keep the law and falling short of God's standard of acceptance and approval. Finally, the people of Israel gave up, and eventually the law God gave them ended by becoming a religion or a god itself. They removed God from their lives and began to worship the law, or they rejected God and His law and worshiped other gods.

The same thing happened to us. Jesus came to give us a kingdom, but because we were not trained for how to live or administer a kingdom, we turned it into a religion. Then we built buildings that we call "church" to maintain that religion. That religion taught us all kinds of gimmicks and paranoias. Our flesh loves religion because it gives us a false sense of security and make us feel good about ourselves.

When Jesus was born, the announcement from heaven came, "Glory to God in the highest, and on earth peace, goodwill toward men!" (Luke 2:14). Jesus also came to announce the acceptable year of the Lord (Luke 4:19).

***

Religion is about escaping the earth

How do we know if a person is operating under the influence of a religious spirit? They will have no understanding of the kingdom of God, no vision for their futures, their countries, or for planet Earth. Their main goal is to escape the planet as soon as possible.

Religion teaches that God created mankind to live in heaven, but God put us on the earth for a period of time because of sin to prove that we are worthy of heaven. They train people that if they do not prove themselves worthy, God will throw them into hell.

The kingdom is about impacting the earth

Kingdom thinking is all about influencing earth with heaven. God did not create us because He needed our help in heaven. He created us to make the earth look like heaven. That is why Jesus said, "On earth as it is in heaven." We are sent from heaven to earth. People in the Bible were not waiting around to go to heaven; they fulfilled the assignment they were sent for.

Life on earth is not a mistake or the result of sin. It is God's original design and plan for mankind. Our purpose is connected to planet Earth in this life and the next. God sent each one of us here with a specific calling and gifts. When we meet God face-to-face, it would be very unfortunate if we had left this planet without fulfilling that calling.

***

Religion will steal everything God gave us

Because religion causes people to ignore their calling and just wait to be raptured, it creates a lazy attitude toward the earth, its resources, and our potential. It creates a passivity toward what is happening on the earth. The mentality creeps in that there is no reason to really make use of everything God gave, and to take care of the earth as if we are just going to be leaving it behind soon anyway; why even try? The result of this line of thinking causes everything to waste away and we never tap into our full potential or the potential of the amazing resources that God gave us in the earth.

The kingdom uses everything God gave us

When you live in the kingdom, you realize that the earth and the world were framed by Jesus our King. God's kids know that there are no jobs for them in heaven and that their eternal purpose is to rule and reign on the earth. When you wake up to this reality, there is a mandate that cannot be ignored, to take care of the earth, use its resources wisely, and to tap into the enormous potential that is hidden away in each individual person for the kingdom.

***

Religion does things to become something or someone

The bottom line of every religion says that you need to try harder next time. They push having more discipline and more rituals, but those things do not bring lasting results. Religious people keep adding new rules and rituals to their lists of duties so they can look and act very pious.

In the kingdom, you do your assignment because you are someone

In the kingdom, we don't become something or someone based on what we do. We are created as sons, and because we are sons, we do our Father's will.

In the garden of Eden, the first thing mankind was tempted with was to become something that they already were. The serpent told the woman that if she would eat from the fruit of the tree of the knowledge of good and evil, she would become like God. This is the foundation of every religion and philosophy—to deceive and blind people from seeing who they already are, and then instigate them to become what they already are by doing something that they are not supposed to do.

Truthfully, in any religion, no matter how much you do, it will be never be good enough! The woman didn't have to do anything to become like God; she already was like God because she was created in His image and likeness.

***

Religion strives to make God happy by singing and giving

When people are full of religion, they have the feeling that they have to do things in order to have a good relationship with God. They may feel like they have to sing to Him, give a lot of their time or money, and just do things in general to gain God's favor. They might not come out and say that this is what they are doing, but their actions speak for them.

There are all sorts of rituals that people and churches feel they have to do in order to be doing things the right way before God. But doing things will not make you closer to God. Just look at Martha in Luke chapter 10. Jesus reprimanded her for doing so much while her sister, Mary, rested at His feet, which He commended her for.

Adam didn't have to do any rituals to make God happy prior to meeting with Him. God came down every day to commune and fellowship with him in the garden. It was a Father-son relationship.

In the kingdom, you enter into God's rest

Since our works were prepared by God before the world began, all we have to do is to learn to trust Him and follow Him on a moment-by-moment basis. When you *follow* Him, He is the one who is going ahead of you, and He will make the path straight and order your steps. When you arrive at a place or an event, you will know that God was already there waiting for you. That is called entering into His rest.

It is hard for mankind to really find rest in our souls. Since the fall, mankind became "human doings" instead of "human beings." Jesus' invitation to mankind is to come to Him and find rest for our souls. It takes a lot of practice to live from a place of rest. But don't get confused; rest doesn't mean you are not doing anything. It means you are not striving any longer to make things happen or to become someone.

To rest means that you are discovering and doing things that were already prepared for you by God. God is going before you to prepare the way and fight your battles. Then you walk in and enjoy the victory and receive the blessing. That sounds like a good deal to me!

It takes a lot of faith, patience, and understanding to operate from a place of rest. Once you enter into rest, it becomes easier to understand the difference between operating from it and striving or stressing.

**

Religion is all about servanthood

One way you can really tell you are in a religious system is that you are made to feel as though you have to serve all the time. This isn't about giving your time and efforts because you love God so much and want to serve; it's normally coupled with feelings of guilt if you don't serve the way the leaders feel like you should. Many times, you are made to serve in areas that are not where you are gifted or called in; for instance, you might be pressured to serve in the nursery when your real gift is in prophetic ministry.

Religion will work you to the bone in serving—all in the name of God. When the Lord never intended for you to be doing most of the things that you wore yourself out doing. At the end of the day, you won't have the energy to give to the actual calling that God has for you. Be careful when you are in this type of religious system.

The kingdom is about sonship

The kingdom is not only about sonship, but about ruling in your sphere of domain. The religious world teaches about sonship wrongly. They want to make you a son or a daughter of a minister or a preacher. To be honest, that's not sonship, but a new form of glorified religious abuse and slavery. If a preacher or organization calls you their son or a daughter, but it doesn't train and release you to fulfill your kingdom assignment, it is not godly.

Once I met a man in an airplane while flying from Accra, Ghana, to Freetown, Sierra Leone. I saw him reading a particular book written by a minister from Nigeria, and I made a comment about it. He said he is one of the sons of that preacher, who is very well-known in Nigeria.

I wanted to ask him how he became his son—if he has his personal phone number and direct access to the man. I wanted to know whether this preacher made his resources available to him. If not, then he wasn't a son just an admirer or a fan.

A son should have direct access to his father and his resources. People get into this kind of bondage of "spiritual sonship" because of their own insecurities and from a desire to feel significant. They think that if they are connected to some famous preacher, that the same favor and blessings that preacher has will flow into their lives someday, and they will also become famous without knowing the price the famous preacher had to pay to get where he is now. This is wrong thinking.

Jesus is the Son of God. The Father has given all things into His hands and Him the heir of all things (John 3:35; Hebrews 1:2). Through Him we are also sons and daughters of God. We have access to our heavenly Father any time, just like Jesus had access to His Father while He was on the earth. God also made us co-heirs with Christ (Romans 8:17). You do not need to go through any mediators or do any rituals prior to meeting with your Father.

We are invited to come to the throne of grace any time we need help. The whole creation is waiting for the manifestation of the sons of God. Why sons and not for more Christians or for church members? The creation recognizes only the sons of God, not any particular religious or sect group members. You will learn more about sonship later in this book.

***

Religion is all about making it to heaven

Religious people are so heaven-focused, that oftentimes they are no earthly good. For most people, once they are saved, they believe that the next stop is heaven. Why? They only heard the gospel of escaping hell and going to heaven. Many didn't even hear the gospel of salvation, which is about restoring what we lost when Adam fell.

The kingdom is about training people to reign

The number one weakness of the church is that they are waiting to escape this planet. We have become so focused on a building that we call "church" that we've lost touch with what's happening in our cultures, governments, families, and sometimes even in our children's lives.

We are trying to escape from the very place God put us to take care of and manage. They teach that real life begins in heaven. According to them, life here on earth is unimportant and insignificant. That is the fundamental flaw with today's *churchianity*. Because of that shaky foundation, nothing lasting can be built on it, so people don't care about what is happening in their nations. They won't engage in what is happening in their communities or cultures. They avoid everything and try to hide from real life. This is very sad indeed!

***

Religion is doing something for God

I hear people say that they want to live for God or want to serve God after they retire. When I hear that, it sounds like they are thinking that they will be doing God a favor. But what they miss is that their lives were His to begin with! I've heard many say that they want to do things for God, but I can tell that what they mean is that they want to perform some religious duties in an attempt to please God or to earn some reward in heaven.

The kingdom is about fulfilling your purpose

When we operate in the kingdom, we will let God work out His purpose through us. That is the whole reason He sent us to this planet. And when we are moving in our purpose and calling, it is the most satisfying thing ever—way more fulfilling than serving some man-made religious idea of what they think you should be doing. God's design for your life and for everyone's lives around you is meant to operate and work together. His ultimate purpose will be achieved when each person is focused on fulfilling what God has called him or her to do in this world.

***

Religion is a poison and opium for the ignorant

Religion is the opposite of the kingdom. To deceive and blind people from the kingdom of God, the devil came up with the idea of religion. To medicate their ignorance, people try to take pride in their religions.

The kingdom is the solution to every problem

Because the earth and humans were created for the kingdom of God, when the kingdom of God is absent from our lives and the earth, we can only expect problems and chaos. The solution is to bring the earth and our lives back under the domain of God's rule. Once the kingdom is established on the earth, these problems and issues will begin to be solved and there will be peace in places that were once chaotic.

***

Religion is a substitute for the kingdom

More people have been killed because of religion and more wars were fought for the sake of it than any other cause.

The Kingdom is a gift to us from our Father

We were created to live in and expand God's kingdom. It is impossible for humans to live without it. Ever since Adam lost the kingdom, God has been in the process of restoring it to mankind.

***

Religion is a deception

Religion is the greatest deception the enemy ever came up with. When people hear the voice of the religious spirit speaking in them, they misunderstand it, thinking it is the Holy Spirit or God. Once the religious spirit takes over our conscience and will, it becomes the god we worship. From then on, we will mistake the voice of this demon as the voice of God because it is coming from our own consciences.

When this takes place, people will lose the ability to discern between what is of God and what is of the devil. Just look at the Pharisees who thought they were serving God, but instead, they were the servants of the devil. They were fighting against God and His very purpose—all along thinking they were serving God. There are billions of people on earth today who belong to different religions, and they all believe they are serving God, but in reality, they are puppets in the hands of the devil.

There are different levels of deception of the religious spirit. Even apostles can be deceived by the devil in some areas of their lives. Even though Peter was anointed of the Lord, he couldn't discern the heart of God for the Gentiles. God had to shake him up through some visions and trances to open his eyes.

The kingdom is a revelation

Unless we receive the kingdom as a revelation first, we will never understand it, nor will it make any sense to us. Not everyone who says the word *kingdom* understands what it is or lives in it. Adding the word *kingdom* to everything we have been saying and doing doesn't make us people of the kingdom, nor will everything we do become things of the kingdom.

***

Religion is about bondage and fear

Religion brings fear into our lives. Because many are possessed by the religious spirit, they walk around in fear: fear of death, fear of the future, fear of failure, and fear of losing their salvation. It literally paralyzes any forward momentum, and religious people will never attempt to do anything outside the bounds of their normal lives that is permitted by the religious spirit.

The kingdom is about freedom

Jesus said whom the Son set free is free indeed (John 8:36). Only the Son of God can set us free from the bondage of religion and the Babylonian system to fulfill our purpose.

YOU WERE MADE FOR THE KINGDOM!

As you can see, religion causes problems, divisions, wars, mental illness, and disorders in people's lives. The more religious a person becomes, the less productive he or she becomes. The bottom line is that you were not made for religion—you were made for the kingdom.

We are kings, and every king needs a kingdom. We are kingdom builders by design. From the time we wake up until the time we go to bed, we are building kingdoms. The question is: Whose kingdom are we building—God's, our own, or the enemy's?

Once the religious spirit enters a person, he or she loses the ability to think right about anything. They will have a skewed perception about life and the earth. They don't even realize that they were created to be royalty. All they can see themselves as is a slave. This is not what God intended for His children.

We are kings, and every king needs a kingdom. The first and most important shift that has to take place in our lives is to come out of religion and into the kingdom. Only then can we properly make the other important transitions that need to happen, which we will be talking about next.

CHAPTER 2

THE SHIFT—*CHANGE IS HERE*, PART II

SHIFT FROM CHURCH TO FUNCTIONING AS AN *EKKLESIA*

Many think the church age needs to come to an end for the kingdom age to begin. That is not so. The kingdom and the church are supposed to function simultaneously. Jesus brought the message of the kingdom first. Then Holy Spirit brought the kingdom on the day of Pentecost, and the church was birthed that day. One will not work without the other. It is a misconception that the church is waiting for the rapture so that the kingdom age can manifest.

The kingdom manifested on the earth on the day of Pentecost, and on that very day the governing body was commissioned. Jesus was preparing for three years for the arrival of the kingdom and the commissioning of its *ekklesia* on the earth.

We Don't Understand the *Ekklesia*

The reason we believe that the church age needs to come to an end for the kingdom age to begin is because of the wrong dispensational teachings we have received. We have looked at the kingdom as existing somewhere out in the future, and church as something that will only operate for a short time period but, according to the Bible, that is not the truth.

People didn't understand the relationship between the kingdom and an *ekklesia, or the church*, so they separated them like they did with the church and state. They are supposed to work together. If there is a kingdom, there has to be an *ekklesia*. And if there is an *ekklesia*, there has to be a kingdom. The *ekklesia* is there to administer the kingdom; it is the governing body of the kingdom of God.

As long as the kingdom of God is in operation, there will also be an *ekklesia*, or governing body. As you know, the kingdom of God is from everlasting to everlasting. As long as there is God, there will be His kingdom, and as long as the kingdom is in existence, there will be an *ekklesia* as well.

When we say the church age needs to come to an end, it means that the existing structure and function of the religious church system needs to end and we need to start functioning as an *ekklesia*. That is the process we are in right now. People everywhere are leaving churches in droves because they are tired of ritualistic religious Christianity. They are looking for something authentic.

We need to delete the old religious operating system and install the new, and start functioning as an *ekklesia*. That is why God gave us a whole book about the *ekklesia* and how it is supposed to function.

The kingdom is the eternal purpose of God for planet Earth. The nation of Israel and the nation of the church are vehicles through which He accomplishes His purpose. Law, grace, or covenants are operating systems through which He relates with mankind. His purpose remains the same, but the operating systems change from age to age.

Finding Our Purpose

We have to be careful not to get stuck in different operating systems, because our focus should be on the purpose of God. That is where the church went wrong. We got stuck with dispensational teachings, plans, and operating systems and missed out on the *purpose*.

Even now, many people focus on the grace, but they miss out on the purpose, which is the kingdom. God did not bring the people of Israel out of Egypt to give them the law; that was not the purpose. The purpose is clearly stated in Exodus. God wanted them to serve Him as a kingdom of priests (Exodus 19:6). The law was given for their well-being and so they could function properly.

Jesus did not save us to give us grace, either. He saved us through His grace to bring us into His kingdom to restore our original identity and purpose. He came to give us a kingdom. That is the purpose behind the grace of God.

We have the same kingdom purpose; the difference is that God deals with us through His grace so that we don't have to live in fear and serve Him out of fear. We can serve Him with freedom and confidence and accomplish His purpose better than those who lived under the law.

If you look at the state of the church, that is not what we see. We don't even accomplish as much as the people who lived under the law. Our productivity is low because we are living in a spiritually constipated state. We are not even as productive as people who don't believe in any god! Most people are not living under the law or grace; they are somewhere in between.

We have to switch from Mount Sinai to Mount Zion, from visiting earthly Jerusalem to the Jerusalem in heaven (Galatians 4:26; Hebrews 12:22). Mount Sinai was a fearful experience for the people of Israel. Only Moses was allowed to go onto the top of the mountain. Anyone else who touched the mountain was put to death.

In the New Covenant, we all come to Mount Zion, the city of the living God (Hebrews 12:22). We are supposed to operate from Zion. Sinai represented bondage, but Zion represents freedom. True freedom is the freedom to fulfill the purpose and assignment God has for your life. If you are not free to fulfill your God-given assignment, then you are not truly free—it doesn't matter what type of church you are a part of or which country you live in.

In technical terms, the kingdom is the hardware and grace is the software. In the Old Testament, the software was the law. In governmental terms, the kingdom is the country, and grace is the governing system or the type of government.

Church Is Not Biblical

If you talk with the Apostle Peter or Paul about church, they won't have any idea about what you are talking about because they never heard the word *church* in their lifetime! You might be shocked by that. Jesus did not use the word *church* when He said He will build His *ekklesia*. The word *church* was adopted by translators after more than a millennium.

We need to come back to Jesus' original idea that He meant for His body. The sooner we do that, the better it will be for us and the world. God has given me a whole book about the *ekklesia*. I highly recommend you read it.

A church and an *ekklesia* are two entirely different entities. The church is a religious institution and the *ekklesia* is a governing body. They function differently and they exist for two different reasons. The church as we know it today doesn't have very much to do with the *ekklesia* Jesus envisioned building.

When we talk about the end of the church age, we are indicating when the present religious system that we call "church" will come to an end. The true *ekklesia* of God will never cease from its existence on this earth; it will be in operation as long as the kingdom of God is in operation. A kingdom cannot function without an *ekklesia*.

SHIFT FROM THE OLD COVENANT TO NEW COVENANT REALITIES

Though we are in the age of kingdom and grace, many believers are unknowingly still living under the Old Covenant. We need to fully shift or switch from the Old to the New Covenant.

When God made the covenant with the people of Israel through Moses, the Gentiles were not invited. We had nothing to do with that covenant. When God judges us on the final day, He won't judge us based on the Old Covenant. We will be judged based on the New Covenant.

Looking for a Sign

In the Old Covenant, God could not dwell inside people, so they had to build a sanctuary, tabernacle, or a temple for His glory to dwell in. Then they had to play music 24/7 to sustain His presence. In the New Covenant, we become His sanctuary, tabernacle, and temple. The Father, Son, and the Holy Spirit dwell in us. Not only that, but God also put His *kingdom* within us. It is sad that most Christians still have to sing to feel God or His presence. They are not led by the indwelling presence of God; they are looking for a sign or a feeling outside or on their bodies.

That is how the Old Testament saints lived. They had to see a sign or smoke. If you don't sense or feel the presence of God inside you all the time, then there is something blocking that presence, or you might not be truly saved yet.

I find it tragic that many people who grew up in church think they were saved from the time that they were born or from when they were very young. Why? They know all the Christian clichés and church mannerisms. Many times when I minister deliverance, I find out that these people are not saved at all. So I lead them in prayer to receive Jesus into their hearts for the first time, and suddenly they sense a change inside them.

Though these people have been part of a church, there was nothing to prove that they were even saved. There is no sign of any restoration, redemption, or sense of purpose about their lives. They just wandered from one meeting to the next, one chore to the next, one trouble to the next crisis, one prophetic word to another *pathetic* word. They sing and shout and speak gibberish, thinking that it is the Holy Spirit. Demons speak in tongues as well, just to let you know. They are hanging in there until they can fly away to heaven.

Communion with God

If you have no ongoing connection or communion with God in your spirit, I encourage you to double-check the salvation you received. Make sure it is the real one, not a fake religious one you received to escape hell or to receive some material blessings. If you only feel the presence of God when you sing or hear some music, then you are still under the Old Covenant or something is not right with the salvation you received.

Most saints of God have no idea about the difference between the Old and the New Covenants. They live a little bit of the old and a little bit of the new. They don't believe God really loves them or that He has a plan for them. They are just waiting to go to heaven and walk on streets of gold.

These people are often found running around looking for a word from a prophet. They are led by the prophets and not by the Spirit. The Bible says, "For as many as are led by the Spirit of God, these are sons of God" (Romans 8:14).

In the New Covenant, we are supposed to be led by the Holy Spirit. In the Old Covenant, people were led by prophets or signs.

Believe it or not, almost the entire church world still lives in the Old Covenant. They don't enjoy the blessings, healing, peace, joy, kingdom or the indwelling presence of God in their spirit man. They are caught in a fight of dos and don'ts. They fight and argue with each other based on which rules they keep from the Old Testament.

The only time they feel the presence of God is when they sing or when someone plays a particular style of music. That was the case in the Old Testament. I used to be like that for a long time because I didn't know any better. I was doing what everyone else was doing. Thank God for His grace that set me free from the religious spirit and from the curses and bondage of the Old Covenant.

Now, I feel the indwelling presence of God 24/7, and even when I sleep, my spirit is in communion with God. When I wake up, I sense things that God was speaking to my spirit man while I was sleeping. This is one of the New Covenant realities and it is available to every single believer in Christ! Most people just don't realize it.

New Covenant Worship

Jesus did not come asking the Jewish people why they weren't blowing the shofar long and loud enough every morning or why they weren't keeping the feasts or particular sacrifices. He didn't ask them why they weren't building more synagogues in every village. Instead, He commanded them to seek His kingdom first. That is His priority and commitment.

We spend a lot time singing trying to make God happy, thinking that if He is really happy with our singing, then He might come down and do something. What we don't even realize is that when we walk into the building, God walks in with us because He has been living inside of us the whole time. We spend years doing this without even questioning it because we are a people of habit, and old habits are hard to change.

Music has the power to influence our moods. So for most people, the only peace they experience is when they hear a particular kind of music. But they are not living in the kingdom culture, which is righteousness, peace, and joy in the Holy Spirit. Jesus said He left His peace with us (John 14:27). We can tap into His peace without hearing music.

Many are waiting for the third temple to be built in Jerusalem so that they can go there and offer some sort of animal sacrifice or agree with those who will do it, trying to appease God. But the Holy Spirit has been busy building a temple for God for the last two thousand years. That temple is not in Jerusalem or any other place we would expect it to be. We will get into more about that later in this book.

Many people confuse worship with music or singing. They have been taught by the religious spirit that singing is worship, and they have been deceived! I have been misunderstood and criticized by these religious spirits because I write and speak against it. It's okay with me, because someone has to pay the price. The word *worship* appears 198 times in the Bible. Not even one time is it mentioned in relation to singing or music. I encourage you to do a study on it and tell me what you find.

We need to praise Him with music, songs, dance, timbrels, and everything we have for what He has done and when He does something amazing like what we see in the New Testament. We have to determine not to just sing a routine like a parrot because that's what we've been taught all of our lives. The religious spirit and its bondage are so persistent, and they will not be easily broken or leave us.

How to Know if We Are Still in the Old Covenant

There is an easy way to test if someone is still operating under the Old Covenant: when someone does something wrong against us or disobeys us, does it creates anger, wrath, and vengeance toward them?

That was God's reaction when someone disobeyed Him under the Old Covenant. In the New Covenant, when we see someone transgressing or disobeying us, it will create compassion or kindness toward that person. It activates God's grace.

This is what we see in the life of Jesus in the New Testament. He didn't bring fire from heaven to burn anyone to death. He did not give any sickness to anyone. When sinners were brought to Him, He was moved with compassion. When He saw the multitude, He was moved with compassion. When the woman who was caught in adultery was brought to Him by religious leaders who were under the Old Covenant, they wanted to punish her, but Jesus extended His mercy toward her.

We do not see any trace of anger in the father in the parable of the prodigal. When he saw his son, he was moved with compassion and didn't question or scold him about his past. In fact, the opposite happened. The father ran and embraced him in spite of the son's own admission of guilt and shame. That is the same heart God has toward each one of us when we return to Him or ask Him to forgive our sins. He is not looking at us with a strained face, but with love. This parable reveals the heart of God toward His children.

The older brother became angry at his father and the brother. This brother represents the Old Covenant. He couldn't show any kindness toward his brother or accept him back because he felt he had committed an unpardonable sin and deserved punishment. May the Lord give us the same heart that the father had when people betray or offend us!

The second way to know if we are still under the Old Covenant is if we are still in bondage to any sin. The Old Covenant was made to cover sin, not to get rid of it. Under the New Covenant we become free from the dominion and the power of sin.

SHIFT FROM BEING EMPLOYED TO WALKING IN OUR KINGDOM ASSIGNMENT

God sent each of us to this planet to do a specific assignment for His kingdom. Adam was born into his kingdom assignment, and everything He needed to fulfill that assignment was provided to him by God. If kingdom provision is not coming to you, the question is: Are you doing what God sent you down here to do?

What is a kingdom assignment? Your kingdom assignment is the very reason God sent you to this planet. What you are currently doing might not be what you were created to do. That is why God has to call people out from certain professions, businesses, and careers, and then release them to fulfill their calling.

Peter, James, and John had to leave their businesses behind to fulfill their kingdom assignment. Matthew was a tax collector, which was a government job. Luke was a doctor. People fight and bribe to get positions in the government of their countries. There is nothing wrong with being employed if that is what your kingdom assignment is.

When Jesus trained the disciples, He sent them out to experience life in the kingdom and specifically told them not to take any money or extra things with them. Why? He wanted them to experience the provision that was attached to their assignment.

Provide neither gold nor silver nor copper in your money belts, nor bag for your journey, nor two tunics, nor sandals, nor staffs; for a worker is worthy of his food. (Matthew 10:9–10)

Once they came back from their trip, Jesus asked them if they lacked anything. Their answer was "no" (see Luke 22:35). That is a kingdom principle: your provision is connected to your calling in the kingdom.

Your calling, vision, or assignment is the system through which God provides for you in His kingdom. If people are not walking in their calling, then God cannot provide for them. He doesn't drop money from heaven. If you are not walking in your calling, then you are on your own to provide for yourself.

Paul said that those who preach the gospel must live from the gospel (1 Corinthians 9:14). So we have to ask why Paul had a tent-making business to support himself. Didn't he practice what he wrote and told others to do? The reason he had a tent-making business is because he made a vow to himself that he was not going to receive any wages or support from the churches he planted. He decided to work with his own hands instead so that he was not draining funds from these newly planted churches.

> For you remember, brethren, our labor and toil; for laboring night and day, that we might not be a burden to any of you, we preached to you the gospel of God. (1 Thessalonians 2:9)

Many misunderstand this about Paul and use it as an excuse to go and start businesses. They think if Paul could do it, then they can do it too. How do we know if we are working for money or if we are doing our kingdom assignment? If we are working for money, then we are not fulfilling our kingdom assignment. If money is the deciding factor in any venture that we do, then money is our master.

What is a master? A master is someone or something that makes decisions for us, or whose decisions we follow. Who is making the decisions for us about where we live, what we do, and what we buy? Is money making those decisions for us, or are we led by God? If money is the deciding factor, then it is the master we are serving.

According to Jesus, there are only two masters in this life (Matthew 6:24). They are God or mammon. Mammon is the spirit that works behind the monetary system of this world. When we go to a store, if the money in our wallet or purse is making the decision about what we should or shouldn't buy, then money is our master.

We should be led by our Shepherd, Jesus Christ, and His Spirit. When someone comes to salvation, there has to be transition from serving money to serving God, and from being employed to walking in our kingdom assignment—from following the system of this world to living in the kingdom of God.

This life is not about us, what we like to do, or how much money we make. It is about doing the will of the One who sent us. At the end of the day, the reward is only for those who fulfilled their God-given assignment.

Many lost their jobs due to the pandemic. If you or someone you know lost his or her employment, please know that God is giving you an opportunity to discover your kingdom assignment. Don't be dismayed or become discouraged.

God is giving us an opportunity through this pandemic to make that transition. If you are employed for survival, then after you finish your job for the day, you should be working on the side to prepare yourself to be launched into your kingdom assignment. Then, when God says it is time, you will be ready to launch.

Many ministries and pastors around the world are struggling to survive. They entered into ministry because they were taught by the religious spirit that being in ministry is the only way someone could serve God. Some of these pastors need to be released to go into politics, start a business, or to do whatever they are called to do.

Shift from a Religious Organization to Functioning as a Nation

When God called out the people of Israel, He wanted them to be a kingdom of priests and a holy nation. They went and established themselves as a nation. They were made up of twelve distinct tribes, but one nation under God. When they failed to accomplish God's mission, He said that He would take the kingdom from them and give it to another nation that bears fruit. That nation is the church, or the *ekklesia* (Matthew 21:43; 1 Peter 2:9).

The church is supposed to be functioning as a nation in every country. That is what Jesus and Peter called the church to be. He said we are a chosen generation, a royal (kingdom) priesthood, and a holy nation. But religion divided the body of Christ into millions of pieces and we became ineffective and irrelevant to the community and nation we exist in. The devil watches what we do every Sunday morning inside our four walls and mocks us and God. This has to end!

Shift from the World's Economy to Kingdom Economy

This world's economy will collapse sooner or later. I believe once the body of Christ prepares, God will judge the Babylonian empire. As God's children, we are not supposed to depend on this world's economy.

We need to stop working for money and implement systems and processes that will create or generate money. Most people are doing what they are paid for instead of what they were created for. Our lives are not supposed to be spent trying to make money; our whole lives are supposed to be spent doing God's will.

Shift from the World's Education to Kingdom Education

The church is supposed to be the resource center for the entire community. Whatever the community needs, the church should have a service to meet that need. Whatever problems a community may have, the church should have the skill and system to solve that problem. That is how we function as the light of the world and salt of the earth.

The purpose of the world's educational system is to raise up a labor force that will sustain and expand the Babylonian system. Kingdom education is focused on helping people discover their purpose, recognize their identity, and then identify their calling, and gifts so they can be trained and released to fulfill their kingdom destiny.

Through the pandemic, the educational system of this world collapsed miserably. Students were forced to learn from home. This was a perfect opportunity to launch kingdom education, but most were not prepared to do that.

The church building should be the busiest place in the world. However, most church buildings are closed six days a week. That building is the biggest financial investment most congregations will ever make. It should be illegal for churches to remain closed on weekdays.

We have to offer courses on every subject that is beneficial to humanity. The church building should be an educational center for family, youth, people who are going through crisis, etc. We should develop courses on how to discover purpose and offer it to our young people.

We should have courses for preparing people for marriage, manhood, womanhood, how to raise children, financial management, marriage counseling, deliverance, skill development, politics and government, and more. I could go on and on about all the topics that the church could be helping the community with as an educational center.

If we would do this, people would stand in line to get inside the church and sign up for a course. We should offer the most competent and quality courses and services—and people's lives would be changed and touched inside the doors of our church buildings.

We should depend on the world's education only when someone needs a higher education to pursue some specialized knowledge such as medicine, politics, or health. I believe that all the basic and foundational education should be done by the church and through the church.

Right now, our children are educated by public school systems that glorify Satan and his kingdom agenda. Our children spend five days a week in these schools where they are taught everything that is anti-God and is very unbiblical. After all that time all week long, they come to church on Sunday and hear a twenty-minute, watered-down message that does not make any sense to them whatsoever.

Mostly they hear about greasy grace or fire and brimstone. Very seldom do they hear a thing about their purpose or the kingdom of God. And then we wonder why our kids don't want to live for God. This needs to change!

We are forced to believe and adopt the narrative of the Babylonian system about family, marriage, the difference between men and women, raising and educating children, and everything else. The church doesn't even have a voice on any issue. Sometimes, the only voice the church has is the *noise* we make when we come together inside our four walls for an hour or two a week.

Shift from the World's Agricultural System to Kingdom Agriculture

Whatever we need for our livelihoods, we need to produce. Right now, we use everything the world is producing and then go to church and sing that this world is not our home. Or we sing, "Oh, take the whole world, but give me Jesus." I have heard people say the first institution God started was family in the garden. What they don't understand is that God planted a garden way before He started a family.

God established kingdom agriculture to sustain life for the first family. God was the first farmer. The food this world is producing now is killing people, causing disease, and creating new diseases. We neglected our responsibility and gave to the hands of the enemy to produce food for us. Do you think the enemy loves you enough to produce healthy food to keep you on this planet? I don't think so.

Can you imagine trusting your enemy to produce the very food you eat? That's like giving permission to someone to kill us. In a palace, before the king eats his food, it has to be inspected and tasted by trustworthy people who will guarantee it was not poisoned by enemies or spies. When a head of state visits other countries, their food and beverages are inspected to be safe for them to consume. They will often bring their own food and chef with them.

We need to start producing our own food chain and stop depending on the world's system. God wanted food to be our medicine and not medicine to be our food. We are supposed to be eating the food that He created in its original form, not the processed and genetically altered foods that are hazardous to our well-being.

Shift from the World's Products to Kingdom Manufacturing

I just finished reading online news about how many companies in the USA are owned by the Chinese government or nationals. China produces 97 percent of antibiotics used in the United States, and about 80 percent of active pharmaceutical ingredients that are used in American drugs, giving the Chinese government absolute control over potentially life-saving medicine. More than 2,400 major U.S. companies are owned by Chinese firms.

The reason I am saying this is because while the American church is waiting and wailing for another revival, our country is being taken over by foreign entities. I have found that people who are religious are the least productive people on this planet; whether they are Christians, Hindus, or Muslims, it is the same spirit operating behind all these religions.

Something happens to the brain of people who are habitually religious or religiously minded. When the Holy Spirit told me to go back and start reading Genesis again, in obedience I went and started reading from Genesis 1:1: "In the beginning God created heaven and earth." God introduces Himself as the Creator, not as a singer or healer.

Holy Spirit told me, "Abraham, there are two groups of people on earth: producers and consumers." Then He asked me, "Which group does the church belong to?" I won't answer this; I will let the reader answer this for themselves.

We have neglected the first revelation of God in the Bible as the Creator. We are supposed to be imitating Him because we are created in His image and likeness. Then He said to me, "People with products have influence." That is what is happening today in this country and around the world. People who produce food and other necessities decide our fate and future. Producers make decisions for the consumers.

We need to encourage our people to produce and not just consume what the world produces. We want to consume what the world gives us but not take any responsibility to care for the planet or manufacture anything from it ourselves! We need to start taking baby steps to kingdom manufacturing—at least producing some essential things we eat and use daily in our lives and in our homes.

Shift from the World's Definition of Family into Kingdom Family

Believe it or not, everything the church believes and teaches from the pulpit about family and marriage is not from the Bible; it comes from the liberal media, demonized educational systems, and movie producers. We have adopted their belief systems, lifestyles, definitions of marriage, the definition of what it means to be a man or a woman, and every other term we use that defines family and how we live life.

That should have never been the case. We should not allow ungodly forces to decide the definition of marriage and form the mindset of our youth. The majority of our youth are indoctrinated by communistic or socialistic agendas.

The Bible is the only authorized source to teach Christians about family and marriage—not movies, universities, or ungodly liberal organizations that do not even acknowledge the existence of God. We need to spit out the venom they have injected into our veins through media, books, and movies.

Churches are afraid to preach the truth, fearing that it will offend the culture or people, because people's mindsets are formed more by the culture than through the Word of God. They are more conformed to the image of this world, and many are offended when we tell them the truth.

God's original idea for marriage and family is when a man and woman are perfectly joined together as "one," fulfilling their God-given kingdom assignment. There is nothing more beautiful to see than a man and woman who know their unique roles and work in partnership to accomplish a God-given kingdom assignment.

Because of the spirit of independence, rebellion, feminism, and selfishness, marriage became one of the most unbearable burdens on earth. For many, their marriage became silent death sentence instead of blessing. They stuff their pain down, not willing to address it or talk about it. It is time to go back to God's original design for marriage and family life so the next generation doesn't have to go through what we did.

Shift from Nationalism into Kingdom Movement

Every time a move of God happens, with it or just prior to it, the devil will introduce a counterfeit move and instigate and influence people to go after the fake move. When the kingdom movement was about to be released, the devil recognized its timing in the spirit realm and introduced a nationalistic spirit in many countries. Nationalism is a counterfeit to the kingdom of God.

As a result, many countries are at the brink of implosion or a civil war. God loves all nations, and they all belong to Him. Just like each individual is supposed to manifest an aspect of God's kingdom, each nation is also supposed to manifest an aspect of His kingdom and His glory.

Building our country or trying to protect it from falling is not the same as building God's kingdom. When we build God's kingdom, our nations will get blessed because it will affect every area of our lives.

If we die for our country, heaven doesn't consider this as becoming a martyr for Jesus and His kingdom. There is nothing wrong with serving our country or serving in an army. If we die for our country, we will receive honor, a reward from the government of our country. If we die for Jesus, we will receive a reward from heaven.

The people of Israel became very nationalistic—to an extent that they thought and believed God was going to use them to rule the entire world. That is how colonialism was birthed. Powerful nations began to subjugate poor nations and made them their colonies, or even slaves.

God wants to rule the earth, the world, and its nations. He wants everyone to be part of it. Dictators, authoritarianism, and empires were raised and built on a nationalistic spirit. Don't fall for the nationalism that is happening in different countries, thinking that is kingdom or establishing God's kingdom and will on earth.

Every tribe, caste, and race is trying to establish its own countries or nations. God wants the entire human race to come under the umbrella of His kingdom rule and reign under one King, Jesus Christ. That is when true peace and prosperity will manifest.

The people of Israel became very nationalistic and egotistical about their blessing; they didn't like people from other nations. They wouldn't even go into their homes. We see that Peter was hesitant to go into a Gentile's house. Not only that, but the disciples also asked Jesus to bring fire from heaven and destroy them. Then after spending more than three years with Jesus, they asked if He was going to establish a kingdom for Israel in the first chapter of Acts.

Jesus' reply to them was to go to the ends of the earth, across every language, cultural, and racial boundary and be His witnesses. He told them that He was not just their King, but the King of the entire earth and all nations. One of the signs of nationalism brewing in our hearts is that we will look to our political leaders as our heroes and saviors instead of God. We have to remember that we only have one Savior—Jesus Christ.

With nationalism, we look at the leader as our protector or savior and will begin to march behind that person or political party. This is extremely dangerous. When we cross that boundary, God will be forced to step in. In the book of Acts, we see that when king Herod gave a speech, people said it was not a voice of a man, but the voice of a god, and they did not give glory to God. As a result, the judgement of God fell on him immediately and he died (Acts 12:21–23).

We see a similar incident in the book of Daniel when King Belshazzar made a great feast for all of his lords and ordered that they use the gold and silver vessels that were taken from the temple of God, which his father had plundered and brought to Babylon. After he did that, the people began to praise the gods of gold, silver, bronze, iron, wood, and stone and did not give glory to God.

But before they could finish the party, the hand of the Lord appeared on the wall like the finger of a man's hand and wrote the king's sentence. That very night, Belshazzar was murdered. That is the danger of nationalism and hero worship. The message of the kingdom is not about nationalism. It is not about one nation becoming the greatest and the most powerful. It is about Jesus ruling in every area and sphere of society.

God wants us to be a blessing to every family and nation on the earth. We don't rule or lord it over them because we are blessed. We need to uplift and bless them to become what they were created to become.

A screwed-up religious and political system will demand the freedom of Barabbas and march behind him—who was a thief, rebel, and murderer and hand over their real King, Jesus, to be crucified. Why would they want Barabbas instead of Jesus, their Creator? Barabbas promised them a natural kingdom and a nation. He was a nationalist!

Shift from Many Shepherds to One Shepherd

One of the weapons that is used the most by the devil to keep the body of Christ defeated and ineffective is by dividing them into a million pieces. One little town will have two hundred churches and two hundred shepherds. They won't talk to each other or work together to reach the town. Each one is trying to be the best and the greatest. One little group is trying to do what they are all supposed to do together. They are not building God's kingdom—they are building their own little kingdoms.

These are not true shepherds. They are self-appointed, trying to make a livelihood, or appointed by their denomination for a monthly salary. Jesus prayed that His sheep would hear His voice and follow Him so that they become one flock under one Shepherd (John 10:16).

Jesus will not appoint two hundred pastors and twenty apostles in one town. Even in the political world, a city or village will have only one elected leader. The village I grew up in had only one village officer. His office had a sizeable staff to manage the affairs of that entire village and its citizens.

It is the same with God; in every village or city, there will be one who is appointed by God for His kingdom—everyone else is a hireling.

How do you know the difference? Discern and see who is building God's kingdom and who is trying to build the biggest ministry or church in town.

The way that the body of Christ is functioning now is mostly out of order—anybody can appoint themselves to whatever position they want, and nobody wants to submit to anyone. Everybody is their own master and trying to be great in the kingdom.

In many parts of the world, people introduce themselves by which denomination or leader they belong to, or they may introduce themselves by what degrees or titles they have. They won't say anything about Jesus; it is all about their papa and their daddy—that's what they call their leaders. They kicked Jesus out of His kingdom and established their own little kingdoms.

Many are led by their favorite prophet or preacher instead of by the Holy Spirit and hearing the voice of their Shepherd for themselves. We replaced Jesus with these preachers and glory in them instead of glorying in the Lord.

We ministers are vessels through whom God speaks; we have no right to receive any credit. If you are blessed by what I write and speak, I do that because the Lord gave me something to write and to speak. If He doesn't give me anything, then I am just like a dead leaf.

Remember the stories of the kings I mentioned above? If we do not give the Lord the glory that He deserves and instead attribute that to a minister or political leader, then that minister and that leader are in trouble! It will be just a matter of time before something happens to them. Don't let that happen to any minister you admire. Never place them on a pedestal or attribute divinity to them. Never glory in a preacher, but always glory in the God who called that preacher.

Preachers cannot change anyone. We ministers know this very well. If we cannot change our own lives or our own families, then how can we change someone else? It is the Word of the Lord and the Spirit of God that changes people. It is not the eloquence of a preacher that touched your heart, but the anointing of the Holy Spirit that was on their words.

Some people talk more about their favorite preacher than Jesus. They praise, adore, and honor them more than they do the Lord. This is dangerous and it falls under idolatry. If the Lord was not using this minister, you wouldn't go to them or even know about them.

All these preachers will pay the price for it sooner or later. Some of them will depart from this earth prematurely. For others, it will diminish the anointing on their lives. If you are blessed by these books or messages, I want you to know that they were given to me by the Holy Spirit. Give Him all the praise and thanks. I didn't come up with any of this on my own.

I don't want to be a superhero for the body of Christ. We already have one superhero, and His name is Jesus Christ our King. Let's bow our knees and our heads to Him and Him alone. To Him alone belongs all dominion, glory, kingdom, and all power and authority, both now and forever and ever. Amen!

Shift from Functioning as Organizations to Functioning as One Body

The original plan of God for the global church is to function as a nation that is made of kings and priests. The nation of Israel is the blueprint for how the church is supposed to operate. They were made of twelve tribes with various gifts, skills, and callings, all working together as one holy nation and manifesting the kingdom of God.

The church is called a holy nation in the New Testament. We are supposed to function as a nation within the natural nation we are living in and solve its problems. We have a long way to go to get there. Until that happens, we will not be leaving this planet. So, when you hear about a pandemic or natural calamity, don't pack your bags!

The body of Christ needs to be united under one God-given vision and purpose, which is the vision of the kingdom of God. The kingdom of God is the only subject that will unite the body of Christ, not revival, shaking, dancing and no other experience will substitute it.

Right now, the church is blaming governments in every nation for the things they themselves failed to do. The church should have raised up righteous politicians. We should have raised up people to occupy every gate of our nation.

The state and the church (kings and priests) are supposed to be working together to run a nation. They both have their own distinctive roles. When one does not fulfill its responsibility, the other one becomes dysfunctional or crippled. That is what happened in the United States. They separated the church and state; all the church did was preach, sing, and hand out some free canned food and used clothing.

The church was supposed to be raising up judges, Supreme Court justices, presidents, governors, and mayors and release them to do what they are called to do. When the church failed to do that, the enemy used that opportunity and filled those posts with his lieutenants to accomplish his will. When the church finally noticed that, they began to blame the government for what they were doing. It is not the government's fault!

In the beginning, the church started and managed all major universities and Christians were the inventors of new products. They were the judges and gatekeepers of the land. So what happened? Over time, their theology got screwed up and the church lost touch with the earth and what was happening in their nations. They became more heaven-focused and began to function like a rescue ship that goes out to save people from hell and take them to heaven.

I could write more about this, but for the sake of time and space, following are the other areas we need to make this transition. We need to shift:

- From fear to confidence in God. The Old Testament saints served God with fear; we serve God as part of His family, as Father-child relationships.
- From focusing on a building to becoming a living temple.
- From sin-consciousness to having righteousness-consciousness.
- From shame to living in honor.
- From passing judgment to governing. We are not supposed to judge people based on their behavior. Jesus said if we judge, we will be judged by the same measure we meet.
- From singing to true worship in Spirit and in truth.
- From the old wineskin (religion) into the new wineskin (the kingdom).
- From living just to function, to fulfilling our God-given purpose.
- From repeated religious rituals to living and walking in the Spirit.
- From offering sacrifice to becoming living sacrifices.
- From the law to grace.
- From leadership to sonship.
- From trying to become entrepreneurs to discovering our callings.
- From trying to be successful to fulfilling our kingdom assignment.
- From different denominations to becoming one body.
- From just working or being employed to discovering our purpose, calling, and gifts.

May the Lord help us do all of these things!

CHAPTER 3

GOD'S ORIGINAL BLUEPRINT

God has only one master plan, purpose, and design for earth and mankind. He doesn't have a secondary plan or idea for our lives. Whenever He does anything, He refers back to the original blueprint and sticks with it.

When any aspect of our lives deviates from God's original design and blueprint, that aspect of life will not work like it is supposed to and we will have problems in that area.

When marriage deviates from God's original plan, then marriage will not work. If you ask God a question about marriage or family life, He will take you and show you the original plan and will tell you how it was in the beginning. This was His original design for it.

That is what Jesus did when the religious leaders asked Him about divorce. He told them "in the beginning it was not so" (see Matthew 19:8).

Something Is Missing!

If government is not functioning the way it should, that means it has deviated from God's original blueprint He laid out.

If our economy is not working as it should, it means the economy is not working according to God's original plan and design.

If our educational system is not working, it is the same problem. Pick any aspect of our nation, and if you notice any dysfunction, it simply means that it is not functioning according to God's original idea and plan.

If people are sick and dying because of diseases or a pandemic, it means our agriculture and health care system is not working according to God's plan.

We have invented more products and created more luxuries, fun, and entertainment than ever before in the history of the world, but life on earth is in a bigger mess than ever before. In spite of there being more people on the planet, there are more depressed and lonely people than ever.

We have churches on almost every street corner. We have more preachers and believers than in any other time in history. But most people don't know their purpose. More people end their lives because of hopelessness. Something is missing and out of alignment.

What is missing is God's original design for life. We are missing God's kingdom and knowing our purpose in it. We have been living and operating without a blueprint. As a result, we have bought the lies of the enemy and created chaos in every area of life. What would happen if you tried to build a building without a blueprint?

Just Two Chapters

God does not have volumes and volumes of blueprints and designs for life on earth. If we plan to build a building or manufacture a product, we will have pages and pages of blueprints and designs. But God doesn't operate the way we do; He put the entire blueprint for our lives and every aspect of our lives connected to this planet Earth in just two chapters.

God made our lives and His plan for us so simple and plain, but the problem is that we missed it. We are always looking for something deep and something to impress people with because of our insecurity, pride, and ignorance. We are always looking for a sign, and as a result, we screwed everything up.

God's original design for our entire lives has been derived from two simple chapters. Every single book ever written by mankind since the beginning of creation has been produced from or is about those two chapters that God originally wrote.

Every branch of study, every subject, all science, every math equation, genetics, every type of engineering, agriculture, physics, biology—everything originated from those two chapters. Every product that was ever made by man is made by materials created by God.

Mankind is still discovering and studying things God has put in those first two chapters in the Bible. We have not even come close to exhausting it! In fact, we have not exhausted even a single verse. And the church neglected them by saying they are just creation stories. We have taken them and drawn pictures of two naked people holding an apple and standing behind bushes with a snake hanging from a tree. That's the picture that comes to our mind when we think of Genesis 1 and 2, that is our limited understanding of them. All the while, every successful business on earth uses and follows the principles laid out by God in the first chapter of the Bible—*and we had no clue!*

God is a God of purpose, patterns, plans, and principles. When we understand His purpose, the patterns (ways) in which He operates, and the principles He revealed in His Word for us to live by, life will make sense for the first time. We will see that God is very predictable, or that the outcome becomes very predictable. It is easy to understand Him and His ways once we comprehend His original design and blueprint. That's why the wisest man who ever lived on this planet said that there is nothing new under the sun, nothing new on this planet, because this man studied and understood God's purpose, patterns, and principles.

That which has been *is* what will be, That which *is* done is what will be done, And there *is* nothing new under the sun. Is there anything of which it may be said, "See, this *is* new"? It has already been in ancient times before us. (Ecclesiastes 1:9–10)

It All Comes from Genesis 1 and 2

Everything goes back to Genesis chapters 1 and 2. Every parable Jesus shared is about what God created in those two chapters. Every book in the Bible refers back to them.

What we find is that the Bible ends where it began. Revelation chapters 21 and 22 repeat what is said in Genesis chapters 1 and 2. It is very predictable. We have made it very complicated and made a mess out of life!

Just look at how critical these two chapters are to life and everything else in the list below.

- When Jesus said He will build His church, He followed the exact blueprint that God revealed in the beginning. What He told the church is the same exact thing God told Adam in Genesis.

- The message Jesus came to communicate with humanity was the same message God told Adam and Eve. He had nothing new to tell us; in fact, He will never have anything new to tell us.

- Every major doctrine in the Bible is mentioned in those two chapters.

- Every invention and all the discoveries man ever invented in any field are based on those two chapters.

- Every successful business follows the principles God mentioned in the first two chapters. Heaven and earth operate by the laws that God set in motion and revealed there.

- Everything Jesus said was word for word what is mentioned in the first two chapters of the Bible.
- Any time God does something on the earth or in relation to mankind, He refers back to His original design.
- Any type of good literature that mankind has ever written was based on the first two chapters of the Bible.

Now that we know how important Genesis 1 and 2 are, every time we interpret life and look for the meaning of life, we should interpret it in the light of God's original plan and design that was revealed. Otherwise, we will end up with the wrong conclusion and at the wrong destination. The same is true with how we interpret the Scriptures. We should interpret them in the light of God's eternal plan and purpose for mankind and the earth so we do not get into error.

The Interruption

In chapter 3 of Genesis, we see an interruption to God's original plan and design. The species God created and put on earth to fulfill that original plan was deceived by an illegal entity that came from another kingdom. There came a distortion, a little twist, and a detour to God's master plan.

This detour set mankind on a wrong path for the last 6,000 years. But God never changed His mind or canceled His plans concerning our lives and this planet. No—He is on a mission to restore everything. It will be accomplished as soon as mankind cooperates with Him. He is waiting for us, not the other way around.

Every evil or problem we see on our planet today began in Genesis 3. Every religion, type of government, murder, abortion, rape, incest, and injustice we see in our community came because of what happened in that third chapter. To remedy this problem, God has been on a mission to restore mankind back to His original idea and plan, which He revealed in the first two chapters.

Every type of religion—Hinduism, Islam, New Age, Buddhism, Judaism, and every other "ism" (Confucianism, Baha'ism, Zoroastrianism, communism, socialism, capitalism), including Christianity, are all rooted in Genesis 3:4–5. Any religion can be summed up as man's attempt to reach God by their works, or to please or become like a god apart from Him.

> Then the serpent said to the woman, "You will not surely die. For God knows that in the day you eat of it your eyes will be opened, and you will be like God, knowing good and evil." (Genesis 3:4–5)

Man was already like God in every way. The devil hated it, so his goal was for mankind to declare independence from God and His kingdom, and then try to become like God by doing something. That is what the serpent encouraged the woman to do. He told Eve that if she ate the fruit God said not to eat, she would not die because she would become like God.

The whole plan of salvation came because of what happened in Genesis 3. The purpose of salvation is to restore mankind and the rest of creation to God's original design and blueprint.

Salvation came because of the distortion and the disruption that came to the original plan God had for the earth and mankind. Everything God does, whether He heals, delivers, provides, redeems, saves, or restores, is to go back to His original idea and plan.

Likewise, everything Jesus did and accomplished was to redeem and restore what we lost because of what happened in Genesis 3. Jesus' mission was to restore mankind to their original intent and position, and to remind and re-emphasize God's original plan and blueprint by paying the price for our redemption and salvation. That is what Jesus did for more than three years; He preached and taught people the gospel of the kingdom. That was the purpose for which He was sent (Luke 4:43).

Every time God calls someone to do anything, He either calls them to accomplish something He mentioned in the first two chapters of the Bible, or He calls them to restore something that was broken because of what happened in chapter 3.

The rest of the Bible from Genesis chapter 3 has to do with what happened to mankind and the earth as a result of the interruption that came, and God's plan to redeem and restore everything back to His original plan—which is only completed in Revelation chapters 21 and 22.

God never expected any wicked person to be in any position of authority anywhere on this planet ever. Unfortunately, almost every person who holds a position of authority is not righteous.

When we deviate from God's original plan in any area of our lives, family, or nations, we will encounter problems in those areas. The sooner we align ourselves with God's original plan and design, the better and easier our lives will become.

The church's responsibility is to teach people God's original design and plan and restore life and mankind back to it.

What are God's eternal plans and purposes?

Before we go deeper into the abovementioned subjects, it is important to establish certain foundational truths. If the foundation is not right, then nothing else will work right. Below are some foundational truths:

- God created planet Earth to establish His kingdom and His will as it is in heaven.
- God is King and He wants to rule the earth.

- It is God's will and plan to rule this earth through mankind.

- God's purpose and plan in every age remains the same, so the plan He had in Genesis 1 is the same plan He has for us now; He doesn't have a new program for us or the earth.

- God's kingdom is everlasting, and His dominion endures throughout all generations (Psalm 145:13). That means there was not a time from the beginning of mankind when the kingdom of God was not in operation.

- God never intended or expected this earth to function without His kingdom.

Those are the foundational truths we need to build our lives on. I will be giving you plenty of Scriptures to prove everything I am saying, and I would encourage you to do a thorough study on this subject on your own.

The Bible talks about seven of God's eternal plans and purposes in relation to earth and mankind. Get ready, because that is what we will be learning about in the next chapter.

CHAPTER 4

GOD'S SEVEN ETERNAL PURPOSES, PART I

When we study God's purposes, patterns, plans, and principles, we learn that there are seven major purposes He has in relation to earth and mankind. The word *purpose* refers to the original intent or reason for existence.

ETERNAL PURPOSE 1: GOD IS THE KING, WITH A KINGDOM TO ESTABLISH ON EARTH

This is God's eternal purpose, and it is the first and foremost purpose that we need to understand. Every other doctrine and plan is secondary to this major one. Everything God does in relation to earth is to fulfill this single purpose. That is why He created the earth and mankind. When we align ourselves with God's plan and idea for us, life will become meaningful and the earth will begin to function as it supposed to.

Until we align ourselves with God's purpose, life won't work as it should. We will keep waiting for someone to come and rescue us out of our troubles and this planet. Nations are struggling and people are running out of options for their lives.

When Did the Kingdom Age Really Begin?

Recently, I have heard and read from different sources that the church age is coming to an end and that we are entering into the kingdom age. People say these kinds of things because they lack understanding of the kingdom of God and God's eternal plan and purposes.

It is possible for people to get confused when they hear terms like *kingdom age*, *church age*, and *millennial reign*. My intention in this chapter is to clear up those misunderstandings. What is the difference between the kingdom age and the millennial reign? Does the church age need to come to an end for the kingdom age to begin? I will answer these questions shortly.

The kingdom age refers to the period of time in which God decided to rule this planet with His kingdom. So in reality, the kingdom age began the moment God's rule began on this planet, which was in Genesis chapter 1. The millennial reign refers to when Christ will return to rule and reign on earth with His saints for a thousand years.

For God to rule this planet, He needs humans as His partners. An individual, a group of individuals, or a nation God uses to execute His will and purpose for His kingdom is called an *ekklesia*, or what we call "church."

Adam was the first member of God's *ekklesia* on earth. Through Adam, God began to execute His will and purpose on the earth. When Adam fell, the next person God chose or called to accomplish His purpose was Noah. Noah and his family were the kingdom *ekklesia* on earth.

After Noah, God chose Abraham. Whatever God has done on earth since that time has been based on the promise, or covenant, He made with Abraham. Through him, He established the nation of Israel, which was God's *ekklesia* in the Old Testament (Acts 7:38).

God's ultimate plan for choosing an individual or a group of people is that they would become a nation. The church is supposed to function as a nation. That is why Peter calls us a holy nation (see 1 Peter 2:9). But because of self-appointed ministers or ministers without proper training, the church fractured into a million pieces, rendering the *ekklesia* of God ineffective.

When a group of people, a church, or a nation willingly surrenders to the lordship of Jesus Christ and asks Him to come and rule their lives and communities, the rule and reign of God will manifest in their midst. When people live by the ordinances of the King and by the culture of the kingdom of God, the kingdom age will begin (the kingdom of God will manifest) for them from that day onward.

When did God's rule begin on the earth for the first time through mankind? It was in the garden of Eden. The garden of Eden was the physical manifestation of God's kingdom on earth. His will was done in Eden as it is in heaven. Heaven and earth functioned in total unity and oneness and there was no difference between life in Eden and the life in heaven.

As I mentioned above, the kingdom age in relation to mankind began in Genesis chapter 1. When God said, "Let us create man in Our image, according to Our likeness; let them have dominion … over all the earth…" (Genesis 1:26), that is when it began. Man was created to rule the earth in partnership with God.

God never changed His plan concerning us or the earth. Because of man's disobedience, sin came into this world and there was an interruption to God's original plan. But He never *changed* His purpose.

Because of sin, mankind fell from their position of rulership and gave Lucifer the right to rule the earth. So he began to set up his kingdom. God never wanted the kingdom of darkness to be in operation on this earth. It was man's mistake and choice to give away his authority to the devil.

The Purpose Remains the Same

Ever since the fall, God has looked for humans who would partner with Him to continue His purpose and plan. In some ages, He found only one single human from the entire race to partner with Him, like we see with the lives of Noah and Abraham.

God called Noah and gave him the assignment to build the ark to preserve him and his family, and in turn, the entire human race. When the flood was over and Noah and his family came out of the ark, God told him to do the exact things He told Adam to do in Genesis 1.

Genesis 9:1–2 says,

> So God blessed Noah and his sons, and said to them: "Be fruitful and multiply, and fill the earth. And the fear of you and the dread of you shall be on every beast of the earth, on every bird of the air, on all that move *on* the earth, and on all the fish of the sea. They are given into your hand."

When God called Abraham, He gave him the same assignment. Genesis 12:2–3 says,

> I will make you a great nation; I will bless you and make your name great; and you shall be a blessing. I will bless those who bless you, and I will curse him who curses you; and in you all the families of the earth shall be blessed.

The above verses show rulership. God was going to establish a nation through Abraham to be a blessing to all the families of the earth.

The dispensational teaching messed up our understanding about God's kingdom and purpose. Maybe it was the enemy's plan to introduce the dispensational teaching because it made us believe that

God's kingdom or His rule can't happen during other dispensations and will only manifest during the time of the millennial reign of Christ, so we have to wait until then to see His rule. But the Bible doesn't teach this at all!

For example, people think that during the dispensation of law there was no kingdom and God was not ruling the earth. The Bible teaches God's plan and purpose remains the same throughout all ages. That is what we are going to see from the Scriptures.

Let's see from the Bible what God told the people of Israel during the time of Moses. When God established the nation of Israel, what did He tell them to be and do? We read in Exodus 19:5–6 (KJV):

> Now therefore, if ye will obey my voice indeed, and keep my covenant, then ye shall be a peculiar treasure unto me above all people: for all the earth is mine: and ye shall be unto me a kingdom of priests, and an holy nation. These are the words which thou shalt speak unto the children of Israel.

That is the kingdom of God during the age of law. God wanted them to function as a kingdom by obeying His laws—not just by being ruled by a king, but also ministering to Him as priests.

We Were Made to Rule the Earth

During the time of judges and kings, God had the same plan. When Samuel became old and his sons were not walking in His ways, the elders of Israel came and asked Samuel for a king. He was not happy to hear such a request from people. He went and prayed to the Lord about it.

What the Lord told Samuel is very heart-touching. In 1 Samuel 8:7, the Lord said to Samuel, "Heed the voice of the people in all that they say to you; for they have not rejected you, but they have rejected Me, that I should not reign over them."

God said they rejected Him from reigning over them. The same thing happens today. We can reject God's reign; we can tell Him not to rule over us and our nations and He won't. Because the people requested an earthly king instead of Him, the Lord told Samuel to listen to the people and do what they were asking. Why?

God gave the dominion over the earth to mankind. Man can rule the earth with God or without God. When we try to rule the earth without God, the result will not be good. We will have pandemics, wars, famine, poverty, curse, murder, racism, and religion as a result. Many people put their trust in some presidents and prime ministers to protect and save them. They are rejecting God from reigning over them. They put their leaders (church and political leaders) in the place of God. Things won't go well with such people and nations.

God was sad when people rejected Him as their King. If people can reject the reign of God, I believe people can also invite or welcome the reign of God. Any time a group of people willingly surrender their lives to God and ask Him to reign over them, He will come and set up His kingdom among them and dwell with them.

Jesus Rejected

You might say that the above incident happened in the Old Testament, but that the New-Testament situation is different. However, in the New Testament, things are not much different. People aren't willing to accept the lordship and kingship of Jesus. They want to do their own things and only use God to do things that are beneficial to them.

I want to share with you a similar incident that happened in the New Testament where people rejected God from ruling over them. Jesus Himself shared this in a parable.

> Therefore He said: "A certain nobleman went into a far country to receive for himself a kingdom and to

return. So he called ten of his servants, delivered to
them ten minas, and said to them, 'Do business till I
come.' But his citizens hated him, and sent a delegation after him, saying, 'We will not have this *man* to
reign over us.'" (Luke 19:12–14)

There is another incident in Mark 5 when Jesus went to the land of the Gadarenes and delivered a demon-possessed man. When the people saw what had happened to this man, instead of celebrating and receiving Jesus, they pleaded with Him to leave their region.

Then they began to plead with Him to depart from
their region. (Mark 5:17)

Jewish people did exactly the same with Jesus. He came to them with the good news of the kingdom but it did not sound appealing to them. The devil was not happy about God's kingdom or reign coming to earth.

But they cried out, "Away with *Him,* away with *Him!* Crucify *Him!*" Pilate said to them, "Shall I crucify your King?" The chief priests answered, "We have no king but Caesar!" (John 19:15)

We think that we would never say such things or reject Jesus from ruling over us, right? But if we check our actions and our lifestyles, that is what we tell Him indirectly almost every day. We go to church on a Sunday morning so that we can be blessed. How do Jesus and His kingdom benefit from us going to church every Sunday? Then, Monday through Friday, we work to survive. Almost everything we do is centered on our own efforts to make our lives better.

The Kingdom and the New Covenant

What about the New Covenant? Is it possible for the kingdom to manifest in this day and age? Absolutely! That is what we see with the coming of Jesus.

Jesus came with the message of the kingdom of God. That was the most important subject He preached and taught. He made sure His disciples understood what a kingdom was and how it operated before He introduced the church to them.

When the disciples asked Jesus to teach them how to pray, God's heart was revealed again through Jesus. The whole prayer was about His kingdom, for His kingdom to come and for His will to be done on earth as it is in heaven.

God has not put a time limit on His kingdom manifesting on the earth. Any time people cry out to Him to reign over them, He will do it. The problem is that we are not asking Jesus to reign over us. We have put our politicians in the place of God. We put our trust in them and believe and follow whatever they say. As the Bible says, it is better to trust in the Lord than to put trust in any man or woman. Most people believe what their politicians say more than what Jesus said.

Some nations glory in the strength and might of their army, others in their wealth and influence. God will bring them all down and make sure He rules over the nations and He is in charge. Either we humble ourselves or He will humble us by force.

We see the same thing in the book of Revelation.

> Then the seventh angel sounded: And there were loud voices in heaven, saying, "The kingdoms of this world have become *the kingdoms* of our Lord and of His Christ, and He shall reign forever and ever!" (Revelation 11:15)

The first chapter and the last chapter of the Bible talk about God ruling this planet through us. That's the main theme of the Bible.

> There shall be no night there: They need no lamp nor light of the sun, for the Lord God gives them

light. And they shall reign forever and ever. (Revelation 22:5)

We should not waste any more time waiting for the kingdom of God or the kingdom age to come. We have waited and wasted generations and given everything God gave us to the enemy—and the only thing we did is complain and talk about what the enemy did with what we gave him!

It is God's eternal plan to rule the earth through us. He never told us to take a break from it and He never will. The kingdom age will never expire on this planet. If we do not rise up to our eternal purpose, the enemy will continue to wreak havoc on the earth.

Most believers think they have to die or that the rapture needs to happen for them to start ruling on the earth in their next lives. What they are saying is this life on earth is really a mistake or waste of time and that real life will begin only after we die. That is one of the biggest deceptions and lies of the enemy.

The enemy keeps deceiving believers, illegally ruling this planet by stealing and occupying everything God gave to His children. All the while, these poor believers go to a building on Sunday morning to sing four songs. They think they are doing God a favor by singing four songs to Him and then they wonder why He doesn't show up in their meetings.

They think He showed up because they feel an emotional *kick* without knowing it was the power of music that made them feel better, not God. It has been proven scientifically and physiologically that music has the power to uplift people and even plants. Music can change our emotional moods.

When the feel-good hormone called dopamine gets released into our blood because of soothing music, many misinterpret it as feeling God. But it has been proven scientifically that music influences almost every part of our brains. Music reduces our stress level. For most people, that is the only god (their feel-good hormone) they will experience in their lifetimes. Lord, have mercy!

Any minister or ministry that doesn't equip you to discover and fulfill your purpose is not a legitimate minister or ministry. They are deceitful workers, doing God's work for dishonest gain and for prominence. You need to run from such ministers and churches and never look back. They might be rich or be on TV, by stealing your money by promising you their anointing, favor, or a miracle. Run from such ministers and never give your money to them!

ETERNAL PURPOSE 2: EVERYTHING GOD CREATES SHOULD MANIFEST AN ASPECT OF HIS GLORY AND NATURE

Everything is not god, but everything God created radiates His glory and reveals an aspect of His nature. Everything came from Him or was created by His Word. The heavens declare the glory of God (Psalm 19:1). Everything God created manifests an aspect of His glory. Every creature, plant, earth, heaven, clouds, rain, snow—anything and everything He made or created reveals His glory.

Since the fall, what has happened with mankind is that because they could not see God with their natural eyes, they began to worship things that they could see.

> Professing to be wise, they became fools, and changed the glory of the incorruptible God into an image made like corruptible man—and birds and four-footed animals and creeping things. (Romans 1:22–23)

> For a man indeed ought not to cover *his* head, since he is the image and glory of God; but woman is the glory of man. (1 Corinthians 11:7)

> *There is* one glory of the sun, another glory of the moon, and another glory of the stars; for *one* star differs from *another* star in glory. (1 Corinthians 15:41)

ETERNAL PURPOSE 3: EVERYTHING GOD MADE IN ALL CREATION SHOULD PRAISE HIM

God is an undisputed King. He has no rival. The devil isn't big enough to be considered an enemy of God. We need to give God the honor due unto His name. The verses below explain much better than I can about why and who should praise Him.

> Let heaven and earth praise Him, the seas and everything that moves in them. (Psalm 69:34)

> All Your works shall praise You, O Lord, and Your saints shall bless You. They shall speak of the glory of Your kingdom, and talk of Your power. (Psalm 145:10–11)

> Praise the Lord! Praise the Lord from the heavens; praise Him in the heights! Praise Him, all His angels; praise Him, all His hosts! Praise Him, sun and moon; praise Him, all you stars of light! Praise Him, you heavens of heavens, and you waters above the heavens! Let them praise the name of the Lord, for He commanded and they were created. He also established them forever and ever; He made a decree which shall not pass away. Praise the Lord from the earth, you great sea creatures and all the depths; fire and hail, snow and clouds; stormy wind, fulfilling

His word; mountains and all hills; fruitful trees and all cedars; beasts and all cattle; creeping things and flying fowl; kings of the earth and all peoples; princes and all judges of the earth; both young men and maidens; old men and children. Let them praise the name of the Lord, for His name alone is exalted; His glory *is* above the earth and heaven. And He has exalted the horn of His people, the praise of all His saints—Of the children of Israel, a people near to Him. Praise the Lord! (Psalm 148)

ETERNAL PURPOSE 4: EVERYTHING GOD CREATES MUST WORSHIP OR SERVE HIM AND FULFILL HIS KINGDOM ASSIGNMENT

For by Him all things were created that are in heaven and that are on earth, visible and invisible, whether thrones or dominions or principalities or powers. All things were created through Him and for Him. (Colossians 1:16)

We have confused worship with singing for a long time, and our purpose with worship. Many people are taught in church that God created mankind to worship Him, and they trained them that worship meant singing. So they spent hours and hours singing, trying to make God happy, all along thinking that they are worshiping God.

When anything happens in their nation that they are not happy with, they will gather and sing for a few hours, thinking that might change the situation. Yet while they are singing, some foreigners will come and steal their nation, buy out their businesses, land, and natural resources, and the sons and daughters of those foreigners will end up taking positions in their government and start making demonic policies and decisions for them. Then the people will wonder why their singing didn't make any difference.

Believers have been doing this singing now for a few generations and have almost lost all of their nations and their governments to the devil and his children. Then they shout and bind the devil, thinking he has done something wrong. What they aren't realizing is that the enemy did what we permitted him to do. We handed everything over to him because we didn't want the responsibility of managing what God gave us or understand that this was our purpose, to govern the earth.

God says about our singing, "These people draw near to Me with their mouth, and honor Me with their lips, but their heart is far from Me" (Matthew 15:8). There is no point in saying something with our mouths to God and then going out and doing our own thing or just the opposite. We say we surrender everything, but the moment He asks us to do something or give something, we resist.

We were created for Him; He gave us a free will to choose to serve Him or other gods. We say we love Him, but the problem is that we say that to almost anyone and anything on this planet. When we say we worship only our God, it means we serve Him with all that we have.

I will explain more about worship in a different chapter.

ETERNAL PURPOSE 5: ALL NATIONS AND TONGUES SHOULD SERVE HIM

In both the Old and New Testaments, God has the same plan for nations. He wants them to serve Him and His kingdom purpose. He is not just looking for individuals, but for nations. He wants the individuals that He chooses to eventually become a nation.

> A little one shall become a thousand, and a small one
> a strong nation. I, the Lord, will hasten it in its time.
> (Isaiah 60:22)

In the New Testament, Jesus told us to go and disciple nations. We interpreted it as evangelizing the nations and called it "the Great Commission." We thought God wanted everyone in heaven. But if He wanted us in heaven, He would have kept us there.

Nations are an inheritance given to Jesus. The Father told the Son to ask Him for nations and the ends of the earth would be His inheritance (Psalm 2:8). Jesus wanted nations serving Him. That is what we read in the book of Revelation. Nations that are saved will come and bring their honor to worship Him (Revelation 21:24).

We don't have any nations that are serving Him. Because the church could not believe God for nations, they came up with excuses, saying "nations" meant ethnic groups or language groups. They thought that as long as there are people saved from a particular language or ethnic group, they would find their satisfaction in it. That is not what Jesus meant when He told us to go and disciple nations.

Jesus didn't say, "Go and disciple people *from* every nation." He said, "*of* all nations." This means we are supposed to be discipling nations. People are waking up all over the world and beginning to talk about discipling their nations. That is very exciting!

ETERNAL PURPOSE 6: NO HUMAN SHOULD PERISH AND GO TO HELL

> Even so it is not the will of your Father who is in
> heaven that one of these little ones should perish.
> (Matthew 18:14)

God has a plan for the life of every single person who has ever lived or will live on this planet. Their life was a gift from God. He designed their lives, their shapes, and their sizes to fulfill a specific assignment in His kingdom. The reason this world and the earth are in the shape they are today is because the majority of people don't fulfill what they were sent here to do by God. The world and the earth are missing their contribution.

Most people get stuck in survival mode and live with anxiety and the fear of what might happen if something goes wrong. Many are being cheated and deceived out of their purpose and calling, and live way below their potential and the rights given to them by God.

Today, most human rights and social justice fights are done for freedom from the laws and principles established by God. People fight for abortion, saying it is their freedom to choose. Feminists fight for freedom from being women, wives, and mothers. People fight to change their genders.

> The Lord is not slack concerning His promise, as some count slackness, but is longsuffering toward us, not willing that any should perish but that all should come to repentance. (2 Peter 3:9)

Everything God did and continues to do in relation to the earth and mankind is to fulfill one of these eternal purposes and plans He has. He will never deviate from it. That is why the Bible says that Jesus Christ is the same yesterday, today, and forever (Malachi 3:6; Hebrews 13:8). This means that God's method of operation changes from time to time and from age to age, but His purpose, patterns, plans, and principles never will.

Once you understand His purpose, patterns, plans, and principles, you will understand or know God. But it takes time and effort to learn and understand those things. The next chapter is about the seventh eternal purpose and plan of God for mankind.

CHAPTER 5

GOD'S SEVEN ETERNAL PURPOSES, PART II

ETERNAL PURPOSE 7: MANKIND TO RULE AND REIGN ON EARTH WITH GOD AND ON BEHALF OF HIM

The first and the last chapters of the Bible say the same thing about man's purpose: we were created to rule and reign on earth for all eternity.

> Then God said, "Let Us make man in Our image, according to Our likeness; let them have dominion over the fish of the sea, over the birds of the air, and over the cattle, over all the earth and over every creeping thing that creeps on the earth." (Genesis 1:26)

> There shall be no night there: They need no lamp nor light of the sun, for the Lord God gives them light. And they shall reign forever and ever.
> (Revelation 22:5)

I have written about this more in the book *Discovering the Lost Kingdom*. Please refer to it. But here I am going to say things I could not say in that book.

I am sorry to disappoint you by saying this: Jesus is not building a mansion for you in heaven. I am going to address this issue in this chapter. I waited until this book to say something about it. The last thing the Father instructed Jesus to do was to be seated at His right hand until He makes all of His enemies His footstool (Hebrews 10:12–13).

Our purpose is to rule this planet, or to have dominion over this planet. God never canceled His purpose concerning our lives, and He never will (Revelation 5:10, 22:5). Then you may ask: What about the rapture? What about the mansion Jesus said He is building for us? I am glad you asked those questions.

Is Jesus Building a Mansion for Us?

Jesus said in John 14 that He is going away to prepare a place for us.

> In My Father's house are many mansions; if it were not so, I would have told you. I go to prepare a place for you. And if I go and prepare a place for you, I will come again and receive you to Myself; that where I am, there you may be also. (John 14:2–3)

I wrestled with these verses for a long time to receive a clear understanding about them. I was taught by the religious spirit that Jesus was going away to build mansions for us in heaven. But I couldn't find a single verse elsewhere that says He is involved in some type of construction project in heaven. As far as I know, all the works Jesus had to do were already accomplished or finished.

These are some of the favorite verses of the rapture-waiting believers worldwide. They have been told that Jesus is building some mansions for them, and when they reach heaven, Peter is going to allocate each one their specific mansion. They have been singing and waiting patiently for it for centuries.

The first rule of interpreting the Bible is that we need to interpret Scriptures with other Scriptures. If we remove or take one verse independently from others, we will not receive the whole picture or the meaning that the Holy Spirit wants. Instead, we will go into error.

We should never take a single verse and build a major doctrine out of it or base our entire lives around it. Every doctrine has to be supported by at least two verses that say the same thing. That is where the body of Christ went wrong. Jesus wasn't talking about building a mansion in heaven. He was talking about something else.

There are three key phrases in the verses above that we need to take notice of. They are "in My Father's house *are many mansions*" and "I go to prepare a *place* for you." Then He said, "I will come again and receive you to Myself." The first phrase says *there are* and not there *will be*. That means whatever mansions Jesus was talking about were already in existence when He was saying this.

Then the next questions are: Where is He going? What kind of place is He preparing? When Jesus said He was leaving, the disciples got curious and wanted to know where He was going because they wanted to go with Him. Then the conversation started between them.

Take note that the word *heaven* is not mentioned even once in this entire chapter. That is our preconceived idea. In the following verse, Jesus clearly said where He was going: "Because I go to My Father" (John 14:12).

> Do you not believe that I am in the Father, and the Father in Me? The words that I speak to you I do not speak on My own *authority*; but the Father who dwells in Me does the works. Believe Me that I *am* in

the Father and the Father in Me, or else believe Me for the sake of the works themselves. (John 14:10–11)

We thought Jesus was going to the Father, but in above verses He says the Father dwells in Him, and He is in the Father, and the Father is in Him. So the question becomes: Where did He go, then?

Jesus is in the Father and the Father is in Jesus. He who has seen the Son has seen the Father. Please keep this thought in your heart, even if it sounds confusing for a minute. They are not my words, but Jesus' own.

In verse 6, Jesus said, "I am the way, the truth and the life. No one comes to the Father except through Me." Many people misquote this verse saying Jesus is the way to heaven, but that is not what He said; He said He is the *way* to the Father. Why the Father? Remember, we lost sonship because of the fall of Adam, and now everyone is looking for their Father. We will learn more about this later in this book.

Then the next phrase says He is *going to prepare a place* for us. Then when the place is ready, He is coming again to receive us to *Himself* (not heaven), so we can be with Him. What do those phrases really mean and what did Jesus mean by them? That is what we are going to explore here.

The Father's House

Jesus said, "In my Father's house are many mansions." The first question is where and what is His Father's house? Is there any other reference to the phrase *Father's house* in the New Testament? Another verse says, "My [the Father's] house shall be called a house of prayer for all nations" (Matthew 21:13; Isaiah 56:7).

The Father's house is the place where He dwells. In the Old Testament, it began with Adam; Adam was the dwelling place of God. When he sinned, God could not dwell in man anymore, so He dwelt in a tent called a tabernacle, and then in the praises of His people, and then in the temple in Jerusalem.

Where is our Father's house now? Heaven is God's throne, not His house. The Father's house is where He dwells. Where does our Father dwell now? Let's find that out. Jesus made that very clear in the following verses in John 14. Please read that entire chapter verse by verse when you get a chance.

> At that day you will know that I *am* in My Father, and you in Me, and I in you. He who has My commandments and keeps them, it is he who loves Me. And he who loves Me will be loved by My Father, and I will love him and manifest Myself to him.
> (John 14:20–21)

Then verse 23 is a key verse to understand the *mansion* Jesus said that was in His Father's house. "Jesus answered and said to him, 'If anyone loves Me, he will keep My word; and My Father will love him, and We will come to him and make Our *home* with him.'"

Jesus is saying if we love Him and keep His Word, the Father will love us and They both will come and make Their *home* with us. Notice that word *home*; the Greek word used for *home* here and for *mansion* in verse 2 are exactly the same. In one verse it is translated "mansions" to mislead the reader, and in verse 23 it is translated "home." In the King James Version, the word *abode* is used for *home* in verse 23.

The Greek word used in both of those verses is *mone*, which means "staying, abiding, or dwelling," not "mansion" like the ones we think of by a lakeside! From the beginning of time, it has been God's desire to dwell in us and with us. *Emmanuel* means "God with us." Our bodies give Him the legal right to operate on the earth. In truth, the Father, Son and the Holy Spirit live in us. John chapter 14 talks about this very clearly (see John 14:16, 23).

Those are the only two places in the entire New Testament where the Greek word *mone* is used. It doesn't mean a house or a mansion as we think of, because the Greek word used for house (Father's house) in verse 2 is *oikia*. The word *mone* simply means "a dwelling place" or a place to stay.[1]

The Greek word used for *place* in verse 3 is *topos,* which means "a place, or a portion of space marked and separated from others."[2] Please read the following verses carefully.

Verse 18 says, "I will not leave you orphans; I will come to you." This is the coming He is talking about in verse 3 when the place He is going to prepare is ready. Once the place He is going to prepare is ready, He will come again and receive us to Himself. So that He can be where we are, and we can be where He is. We are in Him, and He is in us (John 14:20).

> A little while longer and the world will see Me no more, but you will see Me. Because I live, you will live also. At that day you will know that I *am* in My Father, and you in Me, and I in you. (John 14:19–20)

At that day? Jesus is talking about the day He is coming to receive us to Himself, when we are in Him and He is in us, which was after a little while—not after two thousand years.

The verses above are talking about the coming of the Holy Spirit that Jesus talked about in verses 16–17. Through the Holy Spirit, the Father and the Son come and make us their dwelling places.

---

[1] Thayer and Smith. "Greek Lexicon entry for Mone". The KJV New Testament Greek Lexicon, accessed Decemner 16, 2020, https://www.biblestudytools.com/lexicons/greek/kjv/mone.html.

[2] Thayer and Smith, "Greek Lexicon entry for Topos," The KJV New Testament Greek Lexicon, accessed December 16, 2020, https://www.biblestudytools.com/lexicons/greek/kjv/topos.html.

> And I will pray the Father, and He will give you another Helper, that He may abide with you forever—the Spirit of truth, whom the world cannot receive, because it neither sees Him nor knows Him; but you know Him, for He dwells with you and will be in you. (John 14:16–17)

When Jesus said, "In My Father's house there are many mansions," it actually means, "In My Father's house, or heart, there are many dwelling places." In turn, humans are His house, and each of us provide Him a dwelling place, or a place for Him to abide.

Jesus is saying that He and the Father and the Holy Spirit will come and make their abode or dwelling with us and in us, and we become the dwelling places, homes, or the *mansions* for them on the earth.

As born-again believers, the Father, Son, and the Holy Spirit are in us. Then Jesus also said that the kingdom of God is within us (Luke 17:21). I hope this makes us understand the value of a human being—who we really are and what we carry inside us.

John 14:28 says,

> You have heard Me say to you, "I am going away and coming back to you." If you loved Me, you would rejoice because I said, "I am going to the Father," for My Father is greater than I.

Right now we are seated in Him in the heavenly places (Ephesians 2:6), so that fulfills what He said in John 14:3: "Where I am, *there* you may be also." We are in heaven and on the earth at the same time—we have dual citizenship. We are spiritual and natural at the same time.

Nowhere else in the Bible do we read that Jesus is building mansions for us in heaven. But the Bible is very clear on where He is and what

He has been doing since He ascended to heaven. There are *seven* verses in the New Testament that say the Father told the Son to be seated at His right hand *until* He makes all of His enemies His footstool. Until that happens, Jesus is not going to get up and do anything. Here is one of those verses:

> But this Man, after He had offered one sacrifice for sins forever, sat down at the right hand of God, from that time *waiting till* His enemies are made His footstool. For by one offering He has perfected forever those who are being sanctified. (Hebrews 10:12–14)

Preparing a Place

Now let us examine the phrase "I go to prepare a place for you." It has been God's desire to dwell in humans from the beginning of time. He created us and gave us a body so that He can receive a legal right to operate in the physical world. God is Spirit, and any spirit without a body is illegal on earth. If any spirit needs to do anything legally on the earth, someone with a physical body needs to give permission.

That is why God created us with physical bodies. We are not our bodies; we are spirit beings living *in* bodies. When we lose our bodies, we become illegal and have to leave the earth. When man sinned, God lost that privilege of dwelling in us. Our sin had to be remitted before God could dwell in us again.

That is why Jesus came. He paid the price and shed His blood on the cross, and the cost of our redemption was paid in full. But that payment has to be remitted in heaven. When Jesus spoke those words in John 14, He was on the earth. He had not returned to His Father yet.

Once He died and rose again, He had to ascend to heaven to present His blood and offer it on the Holy of Holies that is found in the tabernacle in heaven. This was so the Father's demand could be sufficed. We read about it in the book of Hebrews:

> But Christ came *as* High Priest of the good things to come, with the greater and more perfect tabernacle not made with hands, that is, not of this creation. Not with the blood of goats and calves, but with His own blood He entered the Most Holy Place once for all, having obtained eternal redemption. (Hebrews 9:11–12)

At some point, Jesus entered the Most Holy Place in heaven and obtained eternal redemption for us. Until that was done, the Father's requirement was not fully met, and the Father couldn't accept us back as His children—He couldn't make room for us in Him. That is why Jesus said, "I go to prepare a place for you." It meant that He was going to heaven to tell the Father that everything had been accomplished that was required, and it was now okay for Him to make rooms in His heart for His children and for Him to come and dwell in them.

That *place* Jesus mentioned He was going to prepare was the place in our Father's heart. Each one of us has a specific place (room) in the (heart of the) Father. As His sons, each of us is created to reveal a unique attribute, quality, or the nature (image and likeness) of the Father and the Son through the Holy Spirit to the world. That is why He said He and Father will come and make Their home in us in the above verse. The broken relationship between us (His children) and the Father is reconciled through the blood of Jesus.

> Therefore *it was* necessary that the copies of the things in the heavens should be purified with these, but the heavenly things themselves with better sacrifices than these. For Christ has not entered the holy places

> made with hands, *which are* copies of the true, but into heaven itself, now to appear in the presence of God for us. (Hebrews 9:23–24)

> The Spirit of truth, whom the world cannot receive, because it neither sees Him nor knows Him; but you know Him, for He dwells with you and will be in you. I will not leave you orphans; I will come to you. (John 14:17–18)

Jesus is saying again in the verse above that He will come to them. How long was He going to be gone? Jesus was saying He will be coming back to them in a little while, not after two thousand years (John 14:19). If that were the case, those people wouldn't be alive. He was telling them that He would come back to them in a short while. He was talking to the people who were present there.

Jesus came in the Holy Spirit and has been living in each believer, making his or her body His abode or home. Though each of us are now His dwelling place, one person cannot contain and manifest all that God has and is. So He is building a corporate dwelling place—the Bible calls it a temple—by uniting believers one to another. When all the believers in Christ become knit together in love and form a temple for God, only then will this building project be completed.

We are the temple that He has been building for the dwelling place of God through the Spirit. The building project has not been completed yet: Christ in us, the hope of glory (Colossians 1:27). In the New Testament, we are His dwelling place, or temple (1 Corinthians 3:16–17; 6:19–20).

> If it were already completed, we would see the full manifestation of God on earth, but that is not the case. We are fragmented and divided, and God is

grieved by that. He cannot use us to do what He wants to do on the earth. Paul talks about this building. Now, therefore, you are no longer strangers and foreigners, but fellow citizens with the saints and members of the household of God, having been built on the foundation of the apostles and prophets, Jesus Christ Himself being the chief corner*stone,* in whom the whole building, being fitted together, grows into a holy temple in the Lord, in whom you also are being built together for a dwelling place of God in the Spirit. (Ephesians 2:19–22)

For we are God's fellow workers; you are God's field, *you are* God's building. (1 Corinthians 3:9)

Notice the verse above says, "are being built." That means the project is not completed yet and it is still continuing. It will be completed when each believer in Christ comes into full alignment with their kingdom purpose and begins to function where they are supposed to be in His kingdom, joined (knit) together with other believers and becoming one body. That is the job of true apostles and prophets to help each believer find where they belong in the kingdom and to bring the unity of faith among the body of Christ.

Fivefold ministry gifts will be in operation until the following verses are fulfilled.

Till we all come to the unity of the faith and of the knowledge of the Son of God, to a perfect man, to the measure of the stature of the fullness of Christ; that we should no longer be children, tossed to and fro and carried about with every wind of doctrine, by the trickery of men, in the cunning craftiness of deceitful plotting, but, speaking the truth in love, may

> grow up in all things into Him who is the head—Christ—from whom the whole body, joined and knit together by what every joint supplies, according to the effective working by which every part does its share, causes growth of the body for the edifying of itself in love. (Ephesians 4:13–16)

Right now, there is no unity of faith among believers. Each one has their own opinions and is following their own ideas. When the Bible says "Son of God," it's not necessarily talking about Jesus Christ, because in Greek there are no capital or lowercase letters. The translators wrote *Son*, where it was supposed to be *son*, talking about believers. That is also why they used a lowercase *m* for the phrase *perfect man*.

Each of us needs to come to the knowledge of what it means to live as a son of God on the earth. That is the job of the fivefold ministry gifts—to bring believers to the knowledge of their sonship and then how to live as sons in their Father's kingdom. All creation is waiting for the manifestation of the sons of God. Then, once they have manifested, they need to mature to the measure of the stature of the fullness of Christ.

This means that we need to mature until we are able to fully function how Jesus functioned as a Son, or until we all have the same maturity Christ has as the Son of God. Then when we walk on the earth, it will be as if Jesus Himself is walking on the earth again in person. That is why the Bible says as He is in heaven, so are we in this world (1 John 4:17).

There are only a few genuine fivefold ministry gifts in operation today. Not everybody who claims to be an apostle, prophet, or a pastor is called to be one of them. They are impersonators. They have no desire to mature anyone; their desire is to build a big ministry or a church for themselves so they can lord it over poor believers, exploiting their ignorance for their own personal gain.

This is why I always stress that if a minister does not have the desire to see the body of Christ united, then they are not a true minister. If they have no desire to equip you to see where you fit in the body of Christ, find that place for you, and then release you, then they are not called by God.

Believers are like sheep; they go where the shepherds lead them to go. If they are not led, they will go astray. Most believers are stuck and don't know where they fit in the body of Christ. There is a huge task left to help each believer find the right place in the kingdom.

When this "spiritual house" or "holy temple" is ready, the Lord will come and take residence in it—among us—as He did in the Old Testament temple. He is already inside of each believer, and when believers are joined together as members of the same body, then we will see the fullness of Christ manifest among us and through us. That is what God and all creation are waiting for.

This temple is not built by bricks, wood, and concrete, but by living stones. We are all living stones (1 Peter 2:5). Unfortunately, many believers are looking to the Middle East to see some physical temple built there. God doesn't want or require another physical temple on the earth. He is done with that once and for all.

When Jesus said that the temple in Jerusalem would be torn down and not even one stone will remain one upon another in Matthew 24, He literally meant it. He was done with that type of temple; He doesn't desire to dwell in any building made of human hands anymore.

There is one key phrase in Matthew 24:1: "Then Jesus went out and departed from the temple." That was His permanent departure from a man-made structure or temple. He will not return to any such edifice ever. He is waiting for His spiritual temple to be made ready. This new temple, or building, is being built by the Holy Spirit on the earth today. You and I are part of that building.

In the book of Revelation, we read about the future temple:

> But I saw no temple in it, for the Lord God Almighty
> and the Lamb are its temple. (Revelation 21:22)

It was never God's original idea to build or live in a man-made temple. There is a third temple that is being built on the earth today. Let's find out where it is in the next chapter.

CHAPTER 6

THE THIRD TEMPLE

As we read in the previous chapter, the Bible says there is a temple-building project going on in the earth today. That project is going on inside and between each believer in Christ worldwide by the Holy Spirit. This project is of a temple that is being built for God. Even though God dwells in each believer, one person cannot carry, contain, or manifest the fullness of God; it takes the entire human species joined together as one body to manifest His fullness, His creativity, love, wisdom, power, and wealth that are unfathomable.

> [That you] may be able to comprehend with all the saints what *is* the width and length and depth and height—to know the love of Christ which passes knowledge; that you may be filled with all the fullness of God. (Ephesians 3:18–19)

> Till we all come to the unity of the faith and of the knowledge of the Son of God, to a perfect man, to the measure of the stature of the fullness of Christ. (Ephesians 4:13)

The abovementioned task is the responsibility of a fivefold ministry gift. Today, we find that the body of Christ has been divided into millions of pieces because of self-appointed and false shepherds with selfish ambitions. The church is supposed to be built on the foundation of apostles and prophets, but the current church system has been hijacked or kidnapped by pastors.

Pastors are not equipped to train a believer to fulfill his or her purpose and calling; they can only maintain, nurture, and take care of the sheep. They don't have the right tools to equip and release a person to his or her kingdom destiny. Neither can they bring unity into the body of Christ.

Only when all believers come together as *one body* of Jesus Christ will the fullness of God, Christ, and His kingdom manifest on the earth and be made visible to everyone. This is just like how the Israelites lived as one nation under God, though they were twelve distinct tribes. We are supposed to live as one nation (1 Peter 2:9; Matthew 21:43), without borders, under God.

A Predictable God

When Jesus said, "Destroy this temple, and in three days I will raise it up" (John 2:19) to the Jewish leaders, they were shocked and angry. Their response was that it is impossible to build a temple in three days because it took forty-six years to build the temple in Jerusalem. The problem was that they were talking about two different temples.

Jesus was talking about His body being the temple, and the Jewish leaders were talking about the physical building that was in Jerusalem (John 2:21). Jesus was giving them a hint about what He thought about temples. As I mentioned earlier, it has always been the plan of God to dwell inside of *humans*, not buildings.

The Bible is a book of purpose, patterns, plans, and principles. First, God reveals His purpose, and then He shows us a pattern of how life should work, and then He gives us His principles for how to do it.

When you understand God's purpose, what He wants to accomplish, and the pattern (His ways) already revealed in His Word, He becomes predictable.

God revealed His purpose, patterns, principles, and plans in Genesis chapters 1 and 2. Everything we need to know about life on earth is revealed in those two chapters. As we learned earlier, they are God's original design. We messed it up because of the deception of the enemy. God never planned to take mankind off this planet. It's God's eternal plan for mankind to remain on the earth.

It was God's plan to rule the earth in partnership with mankind. When Adam messed it up, God set in motion a process of restoration. The rest of the Old Testament is filled with patterns and the announcement of that restoration through Jesus Christ.

God chose the nation of Israel to fulfill His purpose for the earth and mankind. He wanted them to be a kingdom of priests and a holy nation. He wanted them to be His children and dwell among them.

However, they betrayed Him and rejected His plans. If we take a close look at their lives and how they lived, we will get an idea of how this kingdom life will work for each believer.

When I say that God becomes predictable, what I mean is this: once we understand God's eternal purposes, everything He does is geared toward accomplishing those purposes. He doesn't keep changing His mind based on what man does or doesn't do or what is happening on the earth.

The Old Testament contains books of purposes, patterns, types, and shadows. The New Testament is the fulfillment of those shadows, patterns, and types. God doesn't have a new agenda for mankind and for our planet. He is the same yesterday, today, and forever. It means His purposes and ways never change. We can trust Him!

When God speaks something, it becomes the law. He will not violate or break His own word. That is what makes Him a trustworthy person. If He does not keep His word, then we cannot trust Him. The truth is that His Word is established in heaven forever. Jesus said heaven and earth may pass away, but His Word will never change or become null (Matthew 24:35).

Sadly, the devil knows more than most believers that God will not break His promises, so he tries to take advantage of Him. The devil is an accuser, and whenever we break God's word, he accuses us before God.

When God says He gave the right of rulership of the earth to mankind, the devil knows what that means. Most believers don't understand what it means. The devil tries to seduce mankind and steal that right from them, or to deceive them to partner with him to accomplish his will and evil on the earth.

It Starts with One

God wanted this entire planet to be filled with His glory. He wanted His kingdom and will to be established here as it is in heaven. He wanted the same quality of life in heaven to manifest on the earth.

God started with one man, Adam, and then He started a family. The first family got so messed up that Cain killed his brother. So God chose another family through Abraham. The problem with Abraham's family was that Abraham and Sarah couldn't have any children. God performed a miracle and gave them a son named Isaac.

God always starts with one man; He doesn't give His plans and vision to a group. Through Isaac came Jacob and his twelve sons. Those twelve sons became twelve tribes. Then those twelve tribes joined together to become a nation. There is a divine progression here in the pattern and plans of God.

The pattern is like this: God starts with one man or one body. Then He creates a family from that man, and then many families join together and become a tribe, and many tribes join together and become a nation. Then everyone in the nation joins together, and they are supposed to become the temple for God.

It is supposed to be the same in the church. We are called the body of Christ, not bodies of Christ. Then that body becomes a family of God. Church is called a family. God takes us from our own natural families and makes us part of His kingdom family.

Finding Your Kingdom Family

In the kingdom, you may not fit in your natural family. When you were naturally born, you were born into a family, a nation, a race, and maybe a tribe. When you are spiritually born again, you are also born into a kingdom family, a tribe, a race, and then a nation, which you will find in the kingdom of God.

Joseph didn't fit in with his own brothers. This is the same with Abraham, David, Moses, Jesus, and anyone else who was used by God. God will take you from your natural family and put you in a kingdom family to fulfill your assignment. You will have brothers, sisters, fathers, and mothers in the kingdom family.

This doesn't mean you need to denounce your natural family. Most of the time, once you are blessed in the kingdom and are fulfilling your kingdom assignment, God will use you to bless your siblings and parents, and then your tribe and nation.

Your calling and gifts will be different from that of your siblings, so He will move you out of your natural family and make you part of a spiritual, or kingdom, family where you feel that you belong. You will feel as though you belong in this kingdom family more than in your own natural family.

Until you find your kingdom family, you will feel lonely and left out. You won't know where you belong on this earth. Many will try to fight with their natural families for acceptance. Many will feel rejected by their own family members. You shouldn't fight with your natural family; instead, leave them alone and ask God to help you find your kingdom family. Don't fight for your acceptance anywhere—not in the natural family or in the kingdom family.

If you have to fight or force others to accept you or to receive you, then it is a sign that you don't belong there or you are not yet ready to fulfill your assignment. When you find your kingdom family, it will be a perfect fit for you. It will be a mutual acceptance.

A family in the kingdom is formed by people who have a similar calling or who are called to influence the same sphere of this world. This means that if you are called into the medical world, when you meet people with a similar vision, something resonates in your spirit and in theirs as well. They have the same spiritual DNA as you do.

If you are called into the world of education, people with a similar calling are supposed to function as a family. Then, many kingdom families will join together to make a tribe for the Lord. Each tribe in Israel was gifted to do something specific. One tribe was gifted with farming and agriculture.

Judah was called to govern. Dan was gifted in the area of judging, or the justice system. The name *Dan* means "judge." There was no need for competition as long as they fulfilled their God-given assignment. When they lost their visions and turned away from the Lord, that's when they began to fight each other and argue between different tribes.

The tribes are supposed to come together to form a nation, but they were so scattered that they were not working together. This is what happened in the church; instead of forming different tribes and working together, the church divided into various denominations and fought against each other. Fighting and arguing comes when people lose the purpose and vision that God gave them.

We lost our purpose a long time ago and since then have been running around, fulfilling our own selfish ambitions. Where there is selfish ambition, there is pride, strife, and jealousy. I am shocked when people say outright that they are jealous of your blessing or that they are proud. They don't see anything wrong with such phrases! People think what they are doing and saying is normal because the enemy's deception crept into the church a long time ago.

Building a Temple for God

Once we become a nation, God starts building His temple in and through us. That is the pattern we see in the Old Testament. When they were established as a nation and the kingdom of God manifested in the natural, the idea of building a temple for God emerged in David's heart.

It is God's plan to dwell in us and with us. The difference between the New Testament and the Old Testament is that in the New Testament, the temple is not made of bricks and wood. The third temple is not a physical building; it is composed of living stones by the Holy Spirit. Each believer is compared to a stone that God uses to build this temple. One single stone cannot make up a temple. When thousands or even millions of stones are joined together, they can make a building.

When the worldwide body of Christ is joined together in one purpose—under the kingdom purpose—that is when the full manifestation of God will be revealed among us. So the pattern of God for a nation and becoming a temple would look something like this:

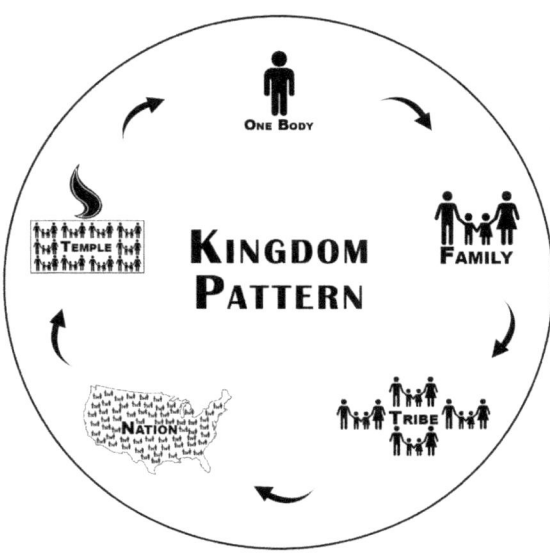

What you see above is the blueprint of God for our planet and humans from the beginning of time. He started with one man, Adam, he was the temple, or the dwelling place, of God on the earth. But one person cannot contain the fullness of God. Then Adam became a family, and then a tribe, and then a nation, and then a temple. When the entire human race becomes part of this temple, that is when we will see the full stature of Christ manifest in the natural (see Ephesians 3:18–19; 4:13).

This is the vision that God gave to this ministry. Through the *ekklesia* and The Kingdom School, He is busy fulfilling this vision in the nations of the world. People everywhere are tired of religion and church as usual. Their spirit man is crying out for the kingdom and to find the family where they feel they belong.

The building project of this temple is not completed yet. It is still going on and we have a long way to go. We read about it again in Ephesians 2:19–22:

> Now, therefore, you are no longer strangers and foreigners, but fellow citizens with the saints and members of the household of God, having been built on the foundation of the apostles and prophets, Jesus Christ Himself being the chief corner*stone,* in whom the whole building, being fitted together, grows into a holy temple in the Lord, in whom you also are being built together for a dwelling place of God in the Spirit.

As I mentioned before, the body of Christ has been so fragmented into denominations by religion. I believe the only message that will unify the body of Christ is the message of the kingdom of God. We've tried everything else, and it didn't work. This message will resonate with those who have the Spirit of God in them.

Unfortunately, the body of Christ is still stuck in the beginning stage of trying to function as a body. We haven't even figured that out yet because we lack the ministry and doctrine of the apostle. Plus, we are fragmented into too many pieces, groups, and denominations, and are fighting for positions and for prominence—and we have a long way to go before we can function as one body as Paul describes:

> And that He might reconcile them both [Jews and Gentiles] to God in one body through the cross, thereby putting to death the enmity. (Ephesians 2:16)
>
> *There is* one body and one Spirit, just as you were called in one hope of your calling. (Ephesians 4:4)
>
> But now indeed *there are* many members, yet one body. (1 Corinthians 12:20)

Only after we figure out how to function as a body can we move into the next stage of functioning as a family. Once we function as a family in Christ, then many families can join together to form a tribe, and then a nation, and then a temple for God to come and dwell in.

> For this reason I bow my knees to the Father of our Lord Jesus Christ, from whom the whole family in heaven and earth is named. (Ephesians 3:14–15)

To start with, each one of us has a part to play in the big picture. We are all living stones that God uses to build this temple with Jesus Christ as the chief cornerstone. (Ephesians 2:20)

The Third Temple Revealed

Then finally we read in Revelation 21:3:

> And I heard a loud voice from heaven saying, "Behold, the tabernacle of God *is* with men, and He will dwell with them, and they shall be His people. God Himself will be with them *and be* their God."

> "But I saw no temple in it, for the Lord God Almighty and the Lamb are its temple." (Revelation 21:22)

This is not the "third temple" people are talking about that is going to be built in Jerusalem in Israel; that is a pseudo-temple to distract believers. God was finished with that type of temple with the death and resurrection of Jesus Christ. When the veil of the temple was torn in two from top to bottom, the Old Covenant and its system came to an end. He is not interested in rebuilding the temple or another veil again.

Then, in 70 AD, the physical temple was torn down as Jesus prophesied in Matthew 24 and the city of Jerusalem was destroyed. That was the end of the Old Covenant age or world. The body of Christ is yet to come to complete grips with that reality. Instead, they are waiting and hoping for another temple to be erected in Jerusalem.

The real temple is what the Holy Spirit is building. It is a spiritual temple built by Him in human hearts and spirits. When that temple is ready, the glory of God will manifest on the earth, and Jesus will come to take His throne and rule this entire planet through us.

We see the same pattern in the Old Testament. When the people of Israel were established as a kingdom of priests, the kingdom of God manifested physically in Israel. This was fulfilled during the time of David. God used him to establish the nation of Israel as a kingdom of priests.

David was a man of war and because of all the blood he had shed in battles and war, God said that his son Solomon would accomplish that dream. The first part of Solomon's reign was the most prosperous time for the nation of Israel.

Solomon built the temple and set everything and everyone in order, and all the people lived as one nation under God. When they began to minister to the Lord, the glory of God filled the temple, and the priests couldn't stand up to minister.

God is in the process of doing the same thing through His church. First, we need to become a nation made of kings and priests as one body under one Shepherd, Jesus Christ. When the worldwide body of Christ becomes united and functions as a nation within their nation—united under one vision of establishing God's kingdom on earth and His will—then heaven will manifest on earth.

When that happens, the glory of the Lord will fill the earth just as the water covers the ocean. This is the dream of God; He will come and dwell among us and with us. We will be in Him, and He will be in us. This is the second coming of Christ that the New Testament talks about. When He comes, He comes to reign. But before He comes, the holy nation and this temple need to be built and ready. We have a long way to go before this can happen!

When Solomon built the temple, he made everything ready according to God's pattern, and put each person and priest in his or her place and function. The priests, the Levites, and every other tribe were in their respective places of responsibility. Only then did the glory of the Lord descend.

Today people are shouting and crying for the glory to fall—but there is no glory. They don't understand the purpose and pattern of God. When we all come into order and align ourselves with the plan of God—each one in his or her respective place and function—nothing will be impossible.

That is the conclusion of the mystery of God:

> But in the days of the sounding of the seventh angel, when he is about to sound, the mystery of God would be finished, as He declared to His servants the prophets. (Revelation 10:7)

CHAPTER 7

THE ORIGINAL DESIGN

When God said, "Let there be light," He was not talking about natural light. He was talking about revelation, understanding, and blueprints.

Every building, project, and product of value starts with a design and blueprint. Everything is done based on that blueprint. Every step of the way, people refer back to it to make sure everything is moving forward according to the plan.

Humans are the most valuable product God has ever created. We come with a manual and a clear blueprint, which are found in the first two chapters of Genesis. Some products man makes, like an airplane or an automobile, come with a huge user manual containing hundreds of pages. God, in His infinite wisdom, included everything about life on this earth in just two chapters.

We Are the Light

God always starts with a blueprint. When God said, "Let there be light," everything in relation to planet Earth was released. The blueprint for every venture, creature, nation, city, book, and product, and invention was released.

We are still tapping into what God released with those four words. There are things that have yet to be made. There are more kingdom cities that need to be built in every nation. There are more inventions waiting to be tapped into and released.

When the Bible says, "Rise and shine for your light has come," it is not talking about natural light. It is saying, "The plan (blueprint) and favor God has for your life has been revealed. The direction you have been waiting for has finally come. Now rise up and walk in it!"

When it says we are the light of this world, it means our lives as believers are the blueprint for people in the world to look at and learn about how life should work on the earth. This is because we have a direct connection with the Creator and they don't. We are the representatives of God and His kingdom.

We should be the solution to every problem this world has. When the world is full of darkness, it is natural for people to look for light. People in the world should be looking to believers to find solutions for their problems.

Unfortunately, it is happening the other way around. Believers are looking to the world and unbelievers for answers and solutions for their problems. Even in marriage, we don't follow the blueprint God gave us in Genesis; we follow the movie version of marriage and family life.

When the pandemic happened, Christians had no clue what to do. They began to look to the world and the ungodly for answers and a cure. That tells me that we have lost our light and saltiness. When the salt loses it saltiness, Jesus said it is good for nothing, only to be thrown out and be trodden by people.

When Jesus was on the earth, He was the light of the world. He was God's blueprint for how life is supposed to work on the earth. The Bible says, "In Him was life, and the life was the light of men" (John 1:4). So, if we want to know what life is, we need to look at Jesus' life and then define it. And that life is the light—or the blueprint—for the rest of mankind.

How He lived and what He did is our blueprint. He came with a definite purpose, and there was a particular place where He had to be during that time. He was not supposed to leave Israel. He was sent to the lost sheep of Israel. As I mentioned earlier, everything and everyone was created for a purpose, and that purpose is connected to a particular place. We simply need to function to fulfill that purpose.

The Purpose Doesn't Change

Every time God creates something, He defines its purpose right then and there. He doesn't wait a hundred years or even a day to tell its purpose. This means that when He creates something, He tells it what He expects that thing or creature to be doing. When He created the sun, He told it to rule the day and give light. That is its purpose. The sun is still doing the exact thing God told it to do in Genesis. You can expect the sun to continue to do the same tomorrow.

When He created the stars and the moon, He told them to rule the night, days, years, and seasons. The stars and moon are still doing the same exact thing today. Unless God tells them to stop, we can expect the moon and stars to continue to do the same tomorrow, next week, next month, and next year.

He created the sea creatures and put them in the water, and they are still in the water today. The purpose of a fish is to swim. They are still swimming in the water and they will be there tomorrow. It doesn't matter how many Darwins come and make up different stories of evolution; those creatures will be in the ocean tomorrow. You can't tell a fish not to swim. If you do, it will ignore you and continue to swim.

When He created the birds, He told them to fly in the sky. That is their purpose. Flight was built into them. That is why birds don't go to school to learn to fly. Fish don't go to universities to learn how to swim faster.

The lion is still the king of the jungle. Try to tell a lion that he cannot be the king of the jungle anymore because Adam fell and he has to wait until the millennial reign of Jesus to rule the jungle—and you will end up as his lunch! Try to tell a bird it cannot fly anymore because Adam fell and sin entered the planet and it will continue to enjoy its flight.

This is a very important thing for us to understand: everything God created is continuing to do what it was created for. Nothing is waiting for the coming of Jesus or millennial reign to do what it was created for.

We Have All We Need

Another important thing to understand is whatever they need to fulfill their purpose has been provided by their creator in the place where He put them, and whatever functions they need to fulfill their purpose were built into them. Whatever the sun needs to produce heat and light was built into it by God. The sun doesn't need to go anywhere to find help.

The sun has not run out of energy or fuel yet. It might in the future when God shuts it down, but for thousands of years it has been producing heat and light nonstop. When it is night in America, it is daytime in Asia; the sun is working nonstop. It doesn't go anywhere to look for energy to burn or even rest. We think the sun is setting every evening and going to rest, but it is not; it is just coming up on the other side of the planet. It is going to continue burning until its appointed time.

In the United States, we get a bill every month for the heat and energy we use. Imagine the amount of energy, heat, and light the sun has been producing all these years. I don't think we can measure it! Everything the sun needs to function and fulfill its purpose was built into it. It doesn't need to go anywhere else or borrow anything.

God made provision for all the sea creatures in the ocean. They have never run out of food. I've never heard of fish going on strike or protesting in the ocean because they were not finding enough food. That would be ridiculous.

What does a fish need to do to find its food? It simply needs to fulfill its purpose, which is to swim. To receive the food it needs, all it required to do is keep its mouth and eyes open while swimming. As long as that fish swims and it remains in the place where God put it, it will never struggle to find its food. Every kind of fish and creature, whatever type of food it needs, is still attached to its place of purpose. Fulfilling our God-given purpose and finding what we need is supposed to be that easy. But we have made it complicated.

How does a bird find its food to live? It simply needs to fulfill its purpose, which is to fly. As long as a bird is free to fly, it will find its food. They don't work for their food. They simply find their food as they do what God created them to do. As long as they continue to do that, they will not struggle or strive for their food. God has prepared each kind of bird to find the type of food it needs.

How do animals in the jungle find their food? The Bible says that God feeds them as they roam on the ground when the sun goes down, and when they are full, they go back to their caves until the morning comes (Psalm 104:20–22).

As long as those animals roam on the ground, they will find their food. They are not worried about finding food or what is going to happen the next day. As long as they are in the place of their domain, food will be there. That is God's covenant to them. When we remove any of these creatures from their natural habitat—the place of their purpose—then we need to feed and care for them.

God does not do home delivery for them. Each creature has to do what it was created to do, and as long as it does, it will find its food and everything else it needs. This is an important kingdom principle.

There are three important things to learn and understand from the above principles. Everything God created has a unique purpose and a specific place to fulfill that purpose. As long as they are in their rightful place and fulfilling what they were created for, their provision is supplied. They never have to worry about their livelihood. This is the master key to understanding kingdom living. If we do not understand the above principle, we will not understand anything about our kingdom purpose or lives.

Just like everything God created has a unique purpose and a specific place to function to fulfill that purpose, human beings are created for a unique purpose and they need a specific place to live and fulfill that purpose. As long as they fulfill that purpose and live in the place God put them, they will not have any problems receiving their livelihood.

When mankind is not fulfilling their God-given purpose and are not living in the place God put them, they will not thrive. Life will not go well for them. They will struggle to survive. That was the case when Jesus looked at people when He was teaching them in Matthew 6.

I have never seen a bunch of birds going on strike against United Nations or World Food Organization because they are not feeding them. God did not appoint the United Nations to feed the birds—or to feed anybody, to be honest!

That is why Jesus looked at human beings who were so worried, tired, hungry, and feeling hopeless, and told them to look at the birds and learn a lesson from them. He said they do not store food in the barns and preserve leftovers. They do not have any freezers or refrigerators to keep food for tomorrow. He said, "Your heavenly Father feeds them" (Matthew 6:26).

God is committed to provide for them as long they fulfill their purpose. He has been doing this for thousands of years. He has a good track record and is proven to be trustworthy. And birds are not complaining; the only creatures that complain and go without food in many places are humans.

Jesus pointed out that the birds are doing what they were created for, and they are being fed and taken care of by our Father. But the people He was talking about, who were created in His image and likeness, were not taken care of. They were worried about what they were going to eat, what they were going to wear, and what they were going to drink—they were struggling to survive.

Jesus also told us to look at the lilies of the field. They don't try hard to become beautiful. They don't need any makeup or artificial colors and parts to appear beautiful; their beauty was built into them. All they need to do to be beautiful is to be authentic and real.

Everything God created in Genesis is still functioning exactly as He told it to. It may not be perfect, but it is fulfilling the purpose for which it was created. God is faithful to provide for them all.

When God created mankind, He made it very clear how He was creating us and why He was creating us—and put us in a particular place—and we missed it! One particular group of people especially missed it and they have been teaching the opposite to their people for so long. All the other people in every language, religion, tribe, and tongue don't have a problem with the assignment God gave them. But we will get to that soon.

Built-In Purpose

Even people who do not believe in God their Creator are naturally fulfilling their purpose. How is this possible? Purpose was built into every human being by their Creator. Our purpose is supposed to be natural for us.

We have to fight hard and go against our very own nature to not to fulfill our purpose. It is like a bird trying not to fly. Can you imagine what that bird would look like and how much it has to struggle to try not to fly? If a bird is not flying, it is apparent that there is something wrong with that bird. If a fish is not swimming, something happened to that fish or it may be dead.

Dogs were created to bark. It does not matter how many times you tell a dog not to bark; after five minutes, when the need comes, that dog will bark again. That is its natural instinct. That dog has to go against its own nature to try not to bark. If a man is not ruling in a particular sphere of domain that means something happened to that individual.

Escape Mentality

When I asked God why it is so difficult for the body of Christ to accept their God-given purpose, this is what He showed me. In 1948, something happened to the body of Christ. When natural Israel became a nation, the body of Christ thought that the end of the world was coming for sure and that the rapture would happen during that generation. They thought that the antichrist and the tribulation were about to manifest.

They believed that the generation who witnessed the rebirth of Israel was the last generation and they would see the return of Christ in their lifetime. Then someone came up with the idea that Jesus was going to come in September of 1988 and wrote a book about it. It became a phenomenon and people quit their jobs thinking the world was going to end. However, that generation, with its preachers, has died and is gone and we are still here.

The New Testament does not teach such doctrines. In fact, the New Testament clearly tells us that the gospel of the kingdom is going to be preached as a witness in every nation, and then the end would come. Nobody seems to be interested in fulfilling that prophecy or the commandment of Jesus Christ (Matthew 24:14).

Misled by this harmful belief, end-time prophetic preachers and teachers came out and poisoned the body of Christ with their *escapetology*. This affected believers worldwide negatively, and they became totally disconnected from their culture. They started to think and act like an estranged species and began to live as parasites.

Nobody focused on his or her purpose and what was happening in their nations. Their sole focus became waiting to *fly out* any minute. The enemy used that opportunity and came in to steal everything God gave to us. As a result, we lost governments, educational institutions, and universities that were once started with the right intention to train and equip citizens to become influential in their communities.

We began to behave like people waiting at the airport for a flight. You cannot get involved with life in an airport while waiting. You can't build anything while you are in transit. That is not the time and place for it. You don't make life's major decisions at an airport—at least, most people don't. You wait until you reach your home or destination. This is how believers who were alive since 1950 have spent their time on earth.

What this *escapetology* did to us is it mutated the gene of those who believed it, and our very DNA began to malfunction as a result. What do I mean by this? What is a mutation? A *mutation* is the change in the structure of a gene that causes variation in the function of a creature and how it lives, based on its belief system or a life-altering event, which will be transmitted to the subsequent generations.

Our wrong belief system altered our DNA and was reprogrammed, and that affected how we lived our lives on earth. Nobody focused on his or her purpose, nor was it talked about. The entire theme became taking more people with us to heaven. That is how the "plundering hell and populating heaven" philosophy became prevalent in some circles.

Because of gene mutation, when children were born to these people, they came with no sense of purpose. The purpose gene was missing from them. They did not care if they fulfilled their purpose or not. Even today, when I talk with many people about their purpose, they just don't care. It doesn't make any sense to them to talk about their purpose.

The rapture and revival theology altered our worldview and what we did with our lives. As a result, the subsequent generations inherited a purposeless and hopeless worldview. They failed to impart hope and purpose to the next generation.

It is amazing to me that people will sacrifice their entire lives for something that is not even mentioned even once in the Bible! Take the words *rapture* and *revival*, for example, which are not even mentioned once in the entire New Testament. But the whole church world is caught up with those two words. At the same time, very few people are interested in something that Jesus taught and preached day and night—which is the kingdom of God. How pathetic is that?

What they did not realize was their theology was incomplete. The enemy took that opportunity and deceived the majority of them, with most living and dying without ever fulfilling their purpose or calling. Now their children and grandchildren are alive, and they don't know why they are here, either. Sadly, we are reaping the consequences of their negligence.

The Damage of Religion

If you try to tell someone from Generation X or Y about their purpose, they will look at you like a deer in headlights. For a vast majority of them, nothing registers with the word *purpose* because the purpose gene is missing from their DNA. But if you tell them about the rapture or revival, they will show more excitement about it.

Recently, I read that only four percent of those in Generation Z have a biblical worldview. If that is true, imagine the condition that the next generation will be in—they will be a totally post-Christian, post-truth, godless generation, like what has happened in Europe.

But if you tell a non-Christian or an unbeliever about purpose and about ruling or reigning on the earth, they will shout and become very excited. Their DNA has not been altered or reprogrammed by religion or a wrong belief system. They were not taught to wait to escape this planet. As I mentioned earlier, it is the natural instinct of a human being to rule on the earth, just like a bird's natural instinct is to fly.

What needs to happen is that believers need to reprogram their DNA according to the Word of God—according to God's original design. This is why we prepared kingdom training materials for children's ministry programs in our churches. We should never show a worldly cartoon movie in Sunday school or as part of our children's or youth ministry program; this will just cause further damage.

The same mutation that happens with the escapist mentality also happens to people who are living under oppressive government systems, such as communism or totalitarianism. We also see it happen to people who endure physical, mental, or religious abuses and traumas. Certain gene or mental faculties are missing in these people. The good news is this can be reversed and reprogrammed with the right training and treatment, so the next generation will not be affected by the mutation and its subsequent dysfunction.

That is why most of the people who invent things or come up with creative ideas are people who do not believe in God or His existence. This may seem strange, but in reality, it makes total sense, because their DNA is in perfect shape when it comes to their purpose and may be mutated in other areas. Their DNA has not been mutated or altered by religion.

Religion is the most damaging and poisonous thing to a human soul and DNA. Nothing destroys a person like religion. I am talking about any type of religion, including "*churchianity*." But nothing brings a person to life more than the kingdom of God and the gospel of the kingdom. It wakes every fiber of a person's being, and for the first time he or she will feel alive and alive for the right reason.

You do not need to be a born-again believer to run a multinational company. You do not need to speak in tongues to invent an airplane. You do not need to pray for three hours every day to invent a space shuttle and go to space or land on the moon. You do not need to be saved to become a president or prime minister of a country, or to become famous in any field or to invent anything. These types of goals and life purpose were built into humans by God; they are part of their God-given purpose, or birthright.

Are You Doing What You Were Created to Do?

If people are not getting fed in any part of the world, then we need to ask if they are doing what they were created for. It is also necessary to find out if they are living in the place God wants them to live. When I say "place," I am not talking about a physical place. I will explain more about that in a minute.

Let's look at how God created us and what He told us to do. Genesis 1:26 is our purpose statement given to us by our Creator. Only the creator or the manufacturer of a product has the right to decide what its purpose is. So it is with humans—only the Creator is able to determine our purpose. If you believe anybody else's idea or teaching about mankind's purpose, you will end up in trouble.

We should not trust a single person on this earth to define our purpose; only our Creator knows our purpose. This is how He created us and what He told us to do:

> Let Us make man in Our image, according to Our likeness; let them have dominion over the fish of the sea, over the birds of the air, and over the cattle, over all the earth and over every creeping thing that creeps on the earth. (Genesis 1:26)

We are created in the image and likeness of God, which means that we have been created to function like God functions. We are God-like creatures created to live in the physical world. God knew that for mankind to live, function, and fulfill their purpose, they also need a place, just like every other creature and thing God has made.

The Bible says the Lord God came down and planted a garden, and then He took the man He made and put him in it. This was called the garden of Eden. Man had everything he needed in the garden.

Man's food, place to stay, and clothing were all provided in the place of their purpose. This means that as long as man stayed in the garden and fulfilled his God-given purpose, he never had to worry about his food, clothing, or accommodations.

But then man was deceived by an enemy kingdom and lost the garden. This garden was not just any type of garden that we know of—this was the kingdom of God manifesting physically on the earth.

God's will was done in Eden as it was in heaven. That is where the kingdom of God was. Where His will and plan are executed and accomplished, His kingdom will manifest. There was no sickness or curse in heaven, so there was no sickness or curse in the garden.

There is no death or strife in heaven, so there was no death or curse in the garden. No poverty or lack in heaven, so there was no poverty or lack in the garden. It was heaven on earth! Or, at least, it was *like* heaven on earth. The same kind of life that is in heaven manifested in the garden.

Mankind was created to live in the kingdom of God and to expand His kingdom on the earth. As long as they fulfilled that purpose, God promised to take care and provide for them.

When we lost the garden, we lost the kingdom of God. When we lost the kingdom, we lost our food. God knew we could not live without a kingdom. The devil also knew that, so he used us and built a pseudo-kingdom, deceiving us with glitter and toys.

Ever since we lost the garden and the kingdom, God has been in the process of restoring His kingdom back to us. That is the message Jesus came with. The first message that came out of His mouth was that people should repent because the kingdom of heaven was near (see Matthew 4:17).

When we rediscover God's kingdom and our assignment in it, Jesus said that everything we need will be added to us. You don't need to work for them; they will come to you.

If you take a fish out of the ocean, you will need to feed it artificially. Why? It is no longer in its place of dominion or purpose. All you have to do to free that fish back to its place of provision is to release it back into the water where it originally belongs, and then it won't be worried about how it will find food.

To free people means to restore them back to where they originally belong and retrain them to do what they were created for. When this happens, they will live just fine. That is why Jesus came—to set the captives free. The enemy kingdom took mankind captive and enslaved people and has been using them to build the devil's kingdom. If someone works for their food and they are not doing what they were created for, then they are not living in God's kingdom; instead, they are working as a slave for another master.

Unfortunately, many believers are still serving the other kingdom because their destinies or kingdom assignments have not been released yet; that aspect of their lives is still being held under captivity. They are satisfied with the mere hope of making it to heaven when they die.

When you take people out of God's kingdom, there is no life or purpose for them. They have to toil with sorrow just to provide for themselves, spending the majority of their lifetime trying to provide their food and shelter. That is what is happening to the majority of people on earth today. Why? They are not living in God's kingdom and not fulfilling the kingdom assignment God has for them.

People are not happy or fulfilled. They depend on all kinds of destructive behaviors, substances, medicines, and addictions to fill that vacuum and to feel fulfilled temporarily. It is so sad that millions even billions of people die without ever discovering God's kingdom or His assignment for them.

It is not rare these days to read about some celebrities who die very young. Some of them are in their twenties and are dying of drug overdoses. They are not doing these things because they don't have fanfare or followers; it's because all along, they were doing something they were not created for. People equate success with money and fame these days. But in God's kingdom, those are not the criteria to decide if someone is successful or not. It is our job to tell them. It is our duty to preach the gospel of the kingdom.

FOUR THINGS THAT ARE ILLEGAL IN THE KINGDOM

It Is Illegal in the Kingdom to Work for Your Food

When Jesus met the disciples at the seashore, they were fishermen. Catching fish was their job, or business. Every day they caught fish to sustain their lives and their families. They were doing that job to make money so that they could buy food.

That is not the way life works in the kingdom. When these men had an encounter with Jesus and His kingdom, they suddenly left their boats and nets, their businesses, and their parents and followed Jesus. It was a radical shift—a total change.

So once they followed Jesus, what did the disciples do to find their next meal? Who provided for them? How did they live and support their families? Jesus and His kingdom became responsible to provide for them from that day until the day they died. Do you remember Jesus telling people to look at the birds and lilies?

When we have an encounter with Jesus—whether we call it salvation, becoming born again, or discovering the kingdom—there has to be a radical change in our lives from that moment on. Unfortunately, that doesn't happen with most people, because they hear the wrong message about going to heaven or escaping hell or other such messages. So they wake up the next morning and continue doing what they have always done to provide for themselves.

Adam did not work for his food. He didn't work for the garden; it was given to him by his Father in order for him to fulfill the kingdom assignment. The reason God gave those things to Adam for free is because the Father wanted him to be fully focused on the assignment He gave him to do. How could Adam focus on his assignment if he had to spend the majority of his time trying to make a living or to find something to eat?

That is what is happening to the majority of people today. They are serving another master to whom they are very loyal because he provides their food for them. It might be a company, a business, or a religious system that they are working for.

In the kingdom, you become diligent to discover your calling, like the disciples, Moses, or anyone else God used. Your calling includes the provision you need to fulfill your purpose. Once you are released to fulfill your kingdom assignment, the King and the kingdom become responsible to provide for you.

> He who did not spare His own Son, but delivered Him up for us all, how shall He not with Him also freely give us all things? (Romans 8:32)

> Now we have received, not the spirit of the world, but the Spirit who is from God, that we might know the things that have been freely given to us by God. (1 Corinthians 2:12)

When it says that if we do not work, we do not eat, it is not talking about doing a job, but rather is speaking about fulfilling the assignment God sent us to do. There is a huge difference between doing a *job* and fulfilling the *work* God sent us. A job is something that we do until we discover our work.

It Is Illegal in the Kingdom to Work for Money

Nobody in a kingdom works for money. They work to fulfill the assignment the king gave them, and they receive money and everything else they need as a reward. Jesus did not do His ministry for money. He did not preach and do miracles so He could take an offering at the end. This was never the case!

But Jesus had someone who handled money among them. Judas was that person. Moses did not go to Egypt to deliver God's people to receive an offering. It is the same for everybody God used in the Bible; money was not the motivating factor for what they did.

There is a difference between doing work and having a job. Your kingdom assignment is your work. When you fulfill your kingdom assignment, money comes to you as a reward. Your motivation should never be how much money you will make. I won't go into this topic too deeply here because I have written about this in detail in my other books.

That is why Jesus told us to seek His kingdom and righteousness first and then all the things we need would be added to us.

It Is Illegal for Anyone to Live in Hunger in a Kingdom

If you live in a kingdom, you are not supposed to live in hunger. If you do, it means you don't have a good king. The king is supposed to make sure everyone in his kingdom is well fed and taken care of. It is his job to protect you from enemies. That is why Jesus was hesitant to send people away hungry. If He did, that wouldn't be a good testimony of Him and His kingdom.

That is why God provided for the Israelites in the wilderness for forty years. If people are living in hunger anywhere on this planet, it means that they are not living in God's kingdom. They will live in hunger only until the day they hear and understand the gospel of the kingdom and how it works.

This is why we must preach the gospel of the kingdom. Many people confuse the kingdom message with the social gospel, thinking that *kingdom* means giving out free food and clothing to poor people. But Jesus did not come to give free food and clothing. Instead, He helped people find their kingdom assignment. He got them away from their mundane jobs and released them to their kingdom destiny.

Life is not supposed to be spent working for food. Life is much more important than the food we eat, and our body is created for something more precious than the clothes we wear (Matthew 6:25).

When people hear the message of the kingdom, they misunderstand it, thinking that the kingdom empowers them to go out and help more poor people. There is nothing wrong with helping the poor; we all must do that. But I want you to see the difference. When Jesus fed the five thousand, it wasn't a program for feeding the poor—they were not all poor people. He didn't do it because He said, "Wow! Look at all these poor fellows who have been following Me for three days. I must give them some food." No!

Jesus fed those people to show everyone that no one should live in hunger in His kingdom. These people had been following Him to learn about His kingdom—they were on a kingdom assignment. He did it to show them a kingdom principle. Unfortunately, people did not understand that; they thought, *Here is someone giving out free bread and fish*, and to them, it sounded like a good deal.

Let's look at what happened after the five thousand people went home once they had been fed. We see that the next day they came looking for Jesus. When they found Him, they tried to make Him their king. They thought if they made Him their king, they would receive free food for the rest of their lives. But Jesus retreated away from them to an isolated place.

If you want to be a king to some people, give out some free food. As long as you give them free food, they will treat you as their king. The moment you stop giving them free stuff, they will strip the crown from you and throw you out.

The kingdom of God is not about giving out free stuff. Every kingdom helps the poor; that is not our purpose. That could be someone's calling. If someone is called to do it, please do it.

In the Kingdom, It Is Illegal to Die Before You Fulfill Your Assignment

Just because something is illegal does not mean that it never happens. Every single human being ever born on this planet is supposed to be spending his or her entire life, energy, gifts, and skills for the expansion of the kingdom of God. You are born as a kingdom builder. But who has time and energy to build God's kingdom today? Everybody is busy taking care of their lives.

We give our energy, skills, and gifts to this world system and serve it with the majority of our time, and for some, with most of their money.

Then at the end, we are left without energy and health—and we cry out to God for Him to heal us and help us. We serve another kingdom with our sweat and blood, making us sick and exhausted—then we come to church crying and asking for healing. How do you think God feels about that? We should have been serving our King from day one.

There are many other things that are illegal in the kingdom of God, like lying, calling your brother a fool, looking at a woman and lusting her in your heart, etc. I am not going to spend time on those things here—just the foundational things that are essentials to the theme of this book.

Changing to Kingdom Thinking and Actions

The more kingdom-minded you become, the more you will understand your relationship with nature and the earth. The more you are detached from God's purpose, the more useless you become to this earth.

Thank God for people like Joseph in the Old Testament. When famine hit Egypt, he didn't blame the end times or climate change. Rather, he came up with a plan to solve the problem. If any nation is facing famine at the moment, the solution to the *famine* is *farming*—not organizing revival meetings or talking about the rapture. They will not solve the hunger problem.

If your nation is facing drought, repentance and planting trees is the solution. If your nation is facing poverty, the solution is to increase people's productivity by helping them discover their purpose, gifts and potential.

Repentance alone will not solve the problem. When we repent, we change the way we think, and when we change our mindsets, we change our actions. Like the Bible says, faith without works is dead (see James 2:26).

If your nation is facing corruption in politics and government, electing righteous people into the authority is the solution. If you don't think there are any righteous people in the political system of your country, then train some righteous people who are called to be involved in government and release them to fulfill their calling. Use time on Sunday morning to train and equip people to fulfill their purpose, rather than trying to entertain them.

If your nation is facing unemployment, then train believers to develop skills to do creative things with their hands. Stop singing more songs in church, and instead use that time to equip the people. Jesus did not start His church to sing on a Sunday morning. Nowhere in the New Testament does it say there has to be an hour of singing before every service—not even once. When will we start obeying what the Bible says and not what our tradition or the religious spirit have taught us?

If your nation or town is facing illiteracy, then use your church building to start an evening school and teach the people in your community how to read and write. Most church buildings remain closed most days of the week. That should never be the case!

If your nation is facing a food shortage, teach your people how to farm and harvest crops. Every family needs to have a garden. It doesn't take that much of a space to have a garden. People can grow vegetables even inside an apartment.

If your town is facing crime issues or drug problems, start a program in the church to teach those young people how to discover their purpose. People steal and kill for the sake of survival. Purpose will give them hope and a reason to be alive other than committing crimes.

Whatever problem there is, the church should have the solution because we are supposed to be the light of this world. That is how we function as the light of this world as Jesus said.

CHAPTER 8

THE POWER OF KINGDOM PURPOSE

As we have seen, whenever God creates something, He defines its purpose, which means He tells it what it is supposed to do, or why He created it, and what He is expecting from it. When God defines the purpose of something, it means that everything it needs to live is attached to that purpose. God will never require something from you if He has not already empowered you to fulfill what He is requiring.

God will never require a bird to fly if He has not built the ability to fly into that bird. He will not require a fish to swim without giving it the ability to swim. That is the way God's kingdom and His ways work.

Remember the parable of the ten minas, or talents? The master gave five to one man, two to another, and one to the next. Then he told them to go and do business with what He gave them. But the person who received only one went and buried his talent in the ground.

When the master came to receive an account of what they did with the talents, he was so angry with the man to whom he gave one because he did not make any effort to do anything with it. The man had a wrong perception of his master. He told him that he was a bad master who wanted to reap where he had not sown.

> Then he who had received the one talent came and said, "Lord, I knew you to be a hard man, reaping where you have not sown, and gathering where you have not scattered seed. And I was afraid, and went and hid your talent in the ground. Look, *there* you have *what is* yours." (Matthew 25:24–25)

The main reason that the master was so angry at this unfaithful servant is because he did not understand how his master operates. Jesus shared this parable to show us how the economy in His kingdom is supposed to operate. He will never require something from you if He has not already made a deposit. If He requires something from you, that means He is confident that you are capable of producing it. You should be happy that He asked you to produce something.

> But his lord answered and said to him, "You wicked and lazy servant, you knew that I reap where I have not sown, and gather where I have not scattered seed. So you ought to have deposited my money with the bankers, and at my coming I would have received back my own with interest. So take the talent from him, and give *it* to him who has ten talents.
>
> "For to everyone who has, more will be given, and he will have abundance; but from him who does not have, even what he has will be taken away. And cast the unprofitable servant into the outer darkness. There will be weeping and gnashing of teeth." (Matthew 25:26–30)

Whatever God created, the power and resources needed to fulfill their purpose has been already built into the very thing or into the environment He put them in. When you plant a seed, everything that seed needs to become a tree is already coded into the seed. The power it needs to absorb the nutrients and water from the soil has been built into that seed. It doesn't need to go to school to learn how to grow and become a tree; as long as that tree stays on the ground, everything it requires to fulfill its purpose is built into it.

We Have to Be in Our "Natural Habitat"

When I went to Kenya, I had the privilege of visiting a natural habitat of wild animals called the Maasai Mara. It was an amazing experience. I saw how the wild animals live, eat, and enjoy their lives where God has put them. I did not see any hungry creatures there. Every one of them was full and satisfied. I did not see any animals complaining, nor did they come to us begging for food.

What if a lion says, "I'm tired of this 'natural habitat.' I'm going to Nairobi to live in an apartment on the fifth floor of a building."? What would happen to that lion? Before long, the lion would die of starvation. Why? It was not created to live in a five-story building in a city. It left the place where it was created to live.

At the same time, I noticed cows that were taken care of by the Maasai people that looked so skinny you could count their ribs. They did not look well-fed because they were not in their natural habitat.

The jungle is the natural habitat for wild animals. Water is the natural habitat for fish. Air is the natural habitat for birds. The ground is the natural habitat for trees. Where is the natural habitat for mankind? You may say this earth, a house, or this world, but that is not correct.

We have plenty of people living on earth who are begging for food. I know many people who are living in houses but struggling to survive. So where do humans belong, and how are they supposed to live?

Everything God created has a purpose, a place, and a function to fulfill that purpose. When one of those things is missing or is out of order, the product will not function as it is supposed to.

When God created Adam, He put him in the garden, which was the kingdom of God manifested physically on the earth. As long as man lived in that place provided by God, he did not lack anything.

Every resource that was required to fulfill man's purpose was provided by God in the garden. If you are struggling to fulfill your purpose, the first question is: Are you living in God's kingdom? If you cannot find the resources you need to fulfill His purpose, you have to wonder if you are living in His kingdom, which is your natural habitat. The second question is: Are you fulfilling your kingdom purpose—the assignment He gave you to do? If not, then you are on your own.

You can either work hard to provide for yourself, or you can live in God's kingdom and fulfill your God-given purpose. Man was created to live in and expand God's kingdom. He is faithful to provide what we need to complete the task He gave us to do.

Your kingdom purpose has power to attract resources, just like a seed has power to absorb what it needs from the ground. Your destiny has the influence to attract other people to you. The moment you begin to live out your kingdom purpose, resources and people who have been waiting to help you will start coming your direction. Until then, they are on standby mode; they cannot come until you start. If you wait for them to come first before you start, it will never happen.

What is Kingdom Purpose?

Everything God created was created for His kingdom and for His purpose. Kingdom purpose is God's original intent for which He created something. God is committed to provide and sustain everything needed to fulfill His kingdom purpose.

Everything He created has a place, purpose, and function. That is why when He talks about the fish He says, "fish of the sea," and when He talks about the birds He says, "birds of the air" because that is where they are supposed to be to fulfill their kingdom purpose.

When something is not in the place where He put it, then it cannot fulfill its purpose and is on its own to sustain and provide for itself. It cannot find what it needs so it has to go into "survival mode" to survive.

If you look around, most people are not in the place where God put them in the beginning. Because of this, they are not fulfilling their purpose and cannot find the resources they need for their livelihood. As a result, they operate in panic and survival mode. That is why when there is a crisis, they tend to hoard things like toilet paper in mass quantities and store them away.

Jesus pointed out that the birds of the air do not store food for tomorrow. Why? They are in the place where God put them, and they are doing what He created them for.

It is not just humans who are not functioning and living in the place where God put them. There were angels that did not keep to their proper abode, or their original place, and rebelled against God.

> And the angels who did not keep their proper domain, but left their own abode, He has reserved in everlasting chains under darkness for the judgment of the great day. (Jude 1:6)

God will show no concern to people, angels, or any other creatures that do not want to be in the place He created and put them. His commitment is to sustain and protect, as long as what He created stays in the place where He wants it and fulfills its purpose.

What if a bird says, "I'm tired of this air; I think I will go live in the water"? There are birds that feed off of the water, but they do not make a nest and live in the water. What if a fish says, "I don't want to live in this water any longer; I am going to jump to the ground or into the next boat that goes by"? What would happen to that fish? It would die or become food for some other creature.

That is what has been happening to mankind for centuries. We said to God, "We don't want to live in your kingdom; we want to do our own thing in our own way. We will appoint kings and presidents and leaders for ourselves and have them rule over us. We will create employment and universities to train people to do those jobs. We don't want Your rule on earth or in our lives. We are not interested in doing Your kingdom assignment." As a result, we created the mess that we see around us and allowed the kingdom of darkness to have free reign in our communities and nations.

The Alternative

For the people who do not want to live in the place God gave them and don't want to do what He created them to do, the devil built an alternative system—a counterfeit kingdom—for them. It is called Babylon, or the kingdom of darkness. In this kingdom, people slave for their master by building his kingdom, and they have to work for their survival.

If you are in Babylon, you will be like the prodigal son who went away from his father's house. In his father's house there was plenty of food, and he did not have to worry about his meals, accommodations, or protection. He did not have to work for it. He did not appreciate the value he was receiving or realize who he was and what he was supposed to do. He thought his father's house was the wrong place to be and that he belonged elsewhere. So he decided to leave his abode and explore outside for himself.

What he found out was not good. This is the situation with most humans. In the parable, this son came back to his father's house where he originally belonged, but most humans do not do that. They die in the pigpen, eating pigs and pig food. When we think of pig food, we think of some menial stuff. It is not so.

Any food that you eat that is not from your Father's house is pig food. Any product that you use that your Father did not produce or create is pig stuff. You might have paid a million dollars for it, but it is still pig stuff because it did not come from your Father's house. *Pig* here represents the devil and his kingdom. Whatever he has to offer you is a counterfeit; the monetary value attached to it or how attractive it looks doesn't matter.

That is why Jesus came and told us to seek His kingdom first—because that is where we originally belonged. We lost it, and He wants to restore it back to us because He knows we cannot live without His kingdom.

Your Birth Was Not a Mistake

Many people tell me that their country is very poor and that they were born in a poor family, so they can't or don't have what it takes to do what God called them to do. They believe they do not have the resources to fulfill their calling. They say these kinds of things because their mindsets were formed by religion and the spirit of poverty that they were born into. They have yet to discover God's kingdom or His kingdom purpose for their lives.

They think God made a mistake by allowing them to be born in such-and-such country and family. They wish to have been born in some other country or in a rich family. But God never makes a mistake. Things will remain the same or get worse for you until you discover God's kingdom.

For the first eighteen years of my life, I slept on a concrete floor. One mat, a pillow, and a bedsheet were all of my earthly possessions. But I only slept on that concrete floor until I discovered God's kingdom and His assignment for my life. By His grace, I discovered it when I was sixteen years old, but it took me two more years to convince my father and to get out of my family's house.

The moment I stepped out to walk in my kingdom assignment, the people and resources God had been preserving for me began to manifest in my life. Actually, God had prepared them for me before the foundation of the world, but they did not come until I made the first move by faith. If you did not hear from God, then there's no faith either—only a presumption.

God used several people to help me get to where I am today, and He continues to use others. I have been used by Him to help others get out of the Babylonian and Egyptian religious systems and to discover God's kingdom and their assignment in it.

The country you were born in and the family or circumstance you were born into was not a mistake, it was all orchestrated by God with meticulous planning! That does not mean that everything was convenient and luxurious where you were born and when you were growing up. Things might be out of order because your parents might not have been living in God's kingdom.

Fighting against God's Agenda

Now the question is: What are you going to do with your life? Are you going to continue the dysfunction, or are you willing to do something about it? Your life is not about yourself; it is about God's kingdom purpose and the next generation. What are you willing to do about them?

We have become selfish; we only care about our own lives and survival. I have discovered that Christians are the most selfish and short-sighted people on this planet. Why do I say that? You might be saying, "Don't we help the poor and do mission work around the world?" We do, but the reason I said we are selfish is because we don't develop our God-given potential or have a plan for the nation we live in. We don't prepare for our next generation. Our vision is limited, and most believers have been waiting to fly away or disappear from this planet. We are like the person who received the one talent. We have the wrong perception of our Father.

Other religious groups have plans for generations to come for who should rule their cities and nations. They already have an agenda for what they want to implement through governments, social organizations, and their educational system; all Christians have planned to do is to take some people out of this planet. They think that they are doing God some kind of favor by teaching people that they will leave the very place God created them for—where He put them to accomplish His will. They deceive these precious people by doing this.

We have been teaching people through our religious system how to escape God's will, purpose, and the place where He put them. Think about that for a minute. We have been training our people how to trespass God's boundaries and agenda. In truth, we are fighting against God and His purpose! It is like someone trying to take the fish out of the water, thinking they are *saving* the fish. No, by doing so, they are killing it.

As I mentioned earlier, God will never demand something from you if He has not made a deposit or investment into you first. This means that He will not ask you to have dominion over the earth if He has not designed you for it. If He is demanding something from you, He knows you are capable of producing it.

God wants whatever He gives you back better and multiplied; otherwise, He won't be happy with you. God has no alternative option for people who do not want to be in the place He created them to be and who misuse the resources He created for His kingdom purpose. There is greater punishment for it than for sins that we think are detrimental.

The Importance of Place

As I mentioned earlier, everything God created belongs to a specific place. The place is important because what is required to fulfill something's purpose is usually found in that place.

That is why our hearts or spirit man is longing to be in a particular place, community, or country. We are like a fish out of water. Have you ever seen it gasping for air? That is the condition of a human spirit that is not living in God's kingdom. We try to pacify that longing with all sorts of fun, entertainment, and sugar, but nothing can substitute God's kingdom. Instead of making our lives better, those substitutes will eventually cause more damage. At the end, our body will get ill, or the spirit man will give up; many end their own lives prematurely. This is a tragedy.

People travel from country to country, city to city, and house to house, trying to find their "home." That search will only be over when they rediscover the kingdom of God, our original home.

Man Was Not Created to Live by Miracles

Life itself is a miracle. The sun shining and hanging in the sky is a miracle in itself. But the sun is doing it because God created it and placed it there. To us, the sun looks like a miracle, but it is just doing what it was created to do. It is a *natural* thing for the sun to do what it was created to do.

Adam was not looking for a miracle every day from God. He was living in the place God wanted him to live. Fish do not live by miracle. People outside of God's kingdom need a miracle and look for a miracle. They need a miracle to bring them to the kingdom. That is why we read about all the miracles in the Bible. Once we arrive in the kingdom, we do not live by miracles anymore.

That is why Jesus told His disciples to go and do miracles and then to tell people that the kingdom of heaven was at hand (Matthew 10:7–8). This tells us that those miracles and signs were not the kingdom, but an announcement of the arrival of the kingdom.

We need to teach people how to live in the kingdom of God. Many Christians are still looking for miracles because they have not discovered the kingdom of God yet. The moment they discover His kingdom, their yearning for miracles will stop as well.

A fish will never run out of food in the ocean. Birds will never run out of air in the atmosphere. Why do we think humans need to go hungry? The only reason is because they are not living in God's kingdom and are not doing what God created them to do.

The Purpose of Miracles

There are several reasons why miracles happen. This is not an exhaustive list, but a few of the main reasons why we see miracles:

- Miracles are an invasion of God's kingdom into enemy territory to cancel out His works or deeds.
- Miracles are a sign of the arrival or the presence of the kingdom.
- Miracles are an act of God to bring us back into kingdom alignment.
- Miracles are bait to bring people into the kingdom of God.
- Miracles are acts of God to restore something back to its original state.

We do not live by miracles in the kingdom. If you need a miracle, then it means something is out of alignment, or an area of your life is operating outside the kingdom and you want God to step in to bring it back into kingdom alignment. Adam was not created to live by miracles because there was a constant supply of resources in His kingdom.

The Importance of Function

Many people get confused about purpose and function. Function is built into something to help fulfill its purpose. People spend all of their time and energy focusing on function, but never fulfill their purpose. Eating, sleeping, and exercising are part of our function, but they are not the reason we exist. Those functions are supposed to help us fulfill our purpose.

Unfortunately, many live only to function, but they are not aware of their purpose. The strangest thing I have found in life is that many people do not care about their purpose. They just live to eat, sleep, and go to work to make some money for their survival—and they keep doing the same thing for decades.

Jesus' Mission

Jesus did not start a soup kitchen in every poor village. He did not train people to start new businesses or tell them to start schools, industries, or anything that we would think of as signs of development or economic growth in a community. He did not create jobs for the jobless.

Jesus had a different message. In fact, when Jesus met a group of businessmen, He did something unthinkable. After just one encounter with Him, these businesspeople left their boats behind—*left their businesses*—and began to follow Him. You might think that was an evil thing to do and would just add more people to the poverty list. But it was not; what He really did was deployed them from their business.

That is opposite to what any earthly government or organization would do. They would not deploy someone from their business; they would help more people start businesses for the economy to grow. That is the way the world's systems and governments work. Then they create an artificial prosperity with material things and people are attracted to it like an insect to a spider web.

Unfortunately, many people who talk about the kingdom think the same way. They believe that creating more jobs, helping the poor with some free food, and training people to start new businesses will advance the kingdom. But it will not. They don't even realize that they are helping the Babylonian system grow instead of the kingdom.

Before we can do all these good works, we need to do something fundamental—something Jesus did for people when they encountered Him. First, He released them to fulfill their kingdom assignment. He helped them discover the kingdom and their assignment in it. That was His priority. Then, He trained them to fulfill that assignment. We should follow the same pattern. If not, all the good things we do will be counterproductive to advancing the kingdom.

To an insect, a spiderweb look likes an elastic swing set, much like a child's trampoline. But what it does not realize is that it is a death trap, and once it gets stuck to that web, that is the end of its life. This is what this world's system does to most people. They are attracted to all the "glittery" things it offers: money, success, fame, luxury, position—the list goes on and on.

They do not recognize that there is a death trap behind all the glitter and deals, and by the time they realize it, it is too late. Unfortunately, many never recognize it because it is wrapped up so well in the deceitfulness of riches and the love of money.

You might try to tell Jesus, "Jesus, you can't add more people to the poverty list by firing people from their businesses and jobs!" Matthew (Levi) was a tax collector, which was a government position. In most countries, it is not an easy thing to get a job in their governments. Matthew may have gone to school to earn a degree in economics or taxation so the government would hire him.

Luke was a doctor, and there he was, running around the world with an apostle. It seems crazy that people would leave their hard-earned educations and jobs. While the whole world longs to have good jobs or to start new businesses, these disciples do something unimaginable like drop their income to follow Jesus around.

How would they support their families? How would their children go to school? Peter was married and I believe he had children. Other disciples may not have been married, but their parents had great expectations for their futures. They most likely believed that when their young sons grew up, they would become the backbone of their families, supporting them financially and taking care of them in their old age.

But those aspirations were thrown out the window when they ran away with a carpenter from Nazareth who promised them some kingdom somewhere that nobody can even see with their natural eyes and who didn't even own a building for His operation. To these parents, their sons would have been considered "runaways."

Once Jesus deployed them from their businesses and jobs, He began to train them to do His kingdom assignment. When they were ready, He sent them out for their practicum. He specifically told them not to take any money, extra clothes or suitcases with them. He said the worker is worthy of his food (Matthew 10:9-10).

Jesus wanted them to experience the kingdom living. He wanted them to know their provision is attached to their assignment. That is a kingdom principle. If something is not practical, then it is not the kingdom of God. Whatever He has called you to do in the kingdom, your provision is attached to it. That is the power of kingdom purpose.

When the disciples came back, Jesus asked them if they lacked anything when He sent them. They said, "No" (Luke 22:35). This is what ministries and churches should be doing for people everywhere, training them to discover their kingdom assignment and then release them to live it. Set them free from the religious and Babylonian system and train them to live in the kingdom of God.

For a person living in a modern world, it will be impossible for them to leave their "boats and nets," because where they live and what they use will be owned by a bank and they will have to make payments every month. It will be difficult for them to leave their jobs because of all the financial obligations and ties. That is why I said this world system is a death trap and once a person gets tangled in it, it would take a miracle to become free from it.

When Jesus taught this, the disciples were shocked and said, "Who then can be saved?" Jesus replied and said, "With men this is impossible, but with God all things are possible." (Matthew 19:25-26)

The Message Has Not Changed

The reason Jesus came preaching the kingdom of God is simple; that is what God has been trying to tell mankind from the very beginning. But they could not understand Him, or they heard something different because the prince of the power of the air put his own twist on it. They did many great things—all except what they were created to do. They built kingdoms, nice gardens, great schools, businesses, libraries, and some built churches and ministries—everything except what He told them to do.

God is a King, and He has a kingdom that He wants to see established on the earth. That is the whole reason He created the earth, created mankind, and then gave that assignment to them. As I already mentioned earlier, Genesis 1 and Revelation 22 show that God has always had the same purpose for the earth and mankind; He is not trying to do anything new. When Jesus came, He didn't have anything new to tell mankind, either. It was the same message that He has been trying to communicate with mankind from the beginning.

There is a huge difference between kingdom business and Christian or worldly business. There is a world of difference between doing a kingdom assignment and being employed in a Babylonian system for survival. The reason Jesus deploys people from their businesses or employment is not because He does not care about their lives, their families, and their livelihoods, or because He wants them to become poor. Why does He do it? He did it because that was not the reason He created them; they were not fulfilling their kingdom assignment. He is releasing them to do their kingdom assignment.

God created each one of us for a kingdom purpose—a kingdom assignment. Every skill we have, all the energy we have, and every day we get to live on the earth is supposed to be invested into one purpose: to build God's kingdom and see His will be done here as it is in heaven.

When you commit yourself to doing that, God makes a commitment to take care of you and to provide for you. You do kingdom business because that is your assignment in the kingdom. If God called you to start a business for His kingdom purpose, then there is nothing wrong with that business. But if you own a business and are not free to fulfill your kingdom assignment, then that business is bondage to you instead of a blessing.

If the job you are doing is your kingdom assignment, then there is nothing wrong with it. But if the job you are doing is keeping you from your kingdom assignment, then that job is not from God. It is from the other kingdom. You need to discover your kingdom assignment and transition into it sooner rather than later.

We only have just enough time to fulfill our kingdom assignment on the earth, so we can't give the majority of our time and lives to the Babylonian system, and then toward the end of our lives try to serve God with the leftovers of our energy and time. God forbid!

We Have a Choice to Make

The freedom Jesus came to give was not external or merely political freedom. That is what the Jewish people wanted in His day. They kept pushing Jesus, trying to force Him to become their king. He rejected it because they did not understand the power of the kingdom that He came to give, and they did not realize that He was already a King.

The freedom Jesus was offering was one that no one else can give or take away—a freedom that enables someone to live in freedom, even in the midst of a very oppressive government or political system. It cannot be taken away even if someone is shut in a prison cell or thrown into a lion's den.

Every soul hungers and thirsts for that type of freedom—one that isn't based on the government, education, or economy of a country, or a business someone runs. The economic freedom that Jesus was offering does not depend on coming from a wealthy family or going to school or a university. None of those factors matter for His kingdom assignment.

That is why these people left their employment and followed Him; and they not only followed Him, but they died for Him and for His kingdom. The disciples did not die for a religion called Christianity. They died for their King and His kingdom.

Jesus did not come to give better employment or political freedom—He came to set the captives free and to release each one to fulfill their kingdom assignment. When each individual fulfills their God-given assignment, development will take place in cities and nations. As a result, everyone will prosper, enjoy freedom, and be in good health.

Do you want to know why the Jewish people asked to release Barabbas and wanted to crucify Jesus? Barabbas was their political leader. He led a revolt against the Roman Empire and was arrested and put in jail. He was a Jewish rebel. But his offer looked more attractive to the people of his day than the offer Jesus was making.

There have always been two options before mankind from the garden of Eden until now, and we have a choice to make. We will either depend on God and His kingdom, or the external freedom and goods of this world's political system.

Barabbas offered political freedom. He offered a better economy for Jewish settlements. He offered better education and free health care systems for the underprivileged. He offered better retirement plans, and protection from Roman soldiers and their oppression. He offered what was appealing to their flesh—but he was a thief, a robber, and a murderer. This sounds like modern-day politicians to me!

Barabbas was a great leader; he was an eloquent speaker and may have been from a reputed Jewish family and tribe. They demanded he be released instead of Jesus because Jesus was offering them a kingdom that they could not see. No free food, no soup kitchens in every poor village, no welfare system, no free housing, no food stamps, no free energy, no free donkeys for the elderly to travel on. They could not understand what kind of kingdom He represented.

To enter this kingdom, you even have to leave what you have. You cannot take your favorite toys with you into the kingdom of God. They will not pass the "scanning machine" and you will be forced to leave them behind.

Another mystery of the kingdom assignment is that you can fulfill it regardless of what type of government you have in your country and which party is ruling. As we see throughout the Bible, government and political systems were not conducive to many kingdom citizens. Regardless, they all fulfilled their calling; Joseph in Egypt, Esther in Persia, Daniel in Babylon, the disciples under the Roman oppression. We need to be free from the political systems of this world and their agendas and persuasions and focus more on fulfilling our God-given assignment.

Why Doesn't God Help Everyone Who Is in Need?

One of the age-old debates is: If God is a good God, then why does He allow people to suffer? Why does He allow evil and not heal all who are sick? There are millions of people who are suffering on this planet.

There are widows, women who are unable to provide for their children, and people crying for a meal or even for a drink of water. Why does God allow such unimaginable suffering on the earth?

Then you read about stories where people receive a miracle from God, like blind Bartimaeus, Naaman the leper from Syria, a woman of Canaan who came for the deliverance of her daughter—who wasn't even Jewish and many others. In the book of Acts, we read about a eunuch from Ethiopia who was traveling through the desert in his chariot. Jesus sent Philip all the way there to meet the eunuch and share the gospel. What makes God move on behalf of certain individuals? Why does God pick certain individuals? God could have sent Philip to share the gospel with the neediest person in Jerusalem, but He did not.

The normal answer that people will give is that these people had a higher level of faith. But there is no evidence that these people possessed a faith that was more special than most people's. One thing I have noticed about our God is that He is committed to His kingdom. He likes to interact with humans only in the basis and context of His kingdom. He has special interest in people who are involved in government.

We see God giving unusual kingdom dreams to heathen kings in the Bible, like Pharaoh in Egypt and Nebuchadnezzar in Babylon. Why would He do that? If you look closely, you will see that all of those dreams were in the context of His kingdom.

The Son of David

Have you ever wondered why Jesus stopped to heal blind Bartimaeus? Let me explain a bit more about this scenario that you might not be aware of. This blind man was not the usual beggar. People called him a blind man, but spiritually he was not blind. He had more revelation about who Jesus was than the most educated religious leaders in the temple.

When Jesus was walking by, this blind man asked others why there was so much commotion going on. They told him that Jesus of Nazareth was passing by. Immediately, something exploded in his spirit man. He did not call Him "Jesus of Nazareth," but cried out and called him "Jesus, Son of David" (Mark 10:47b).

This blind man understood something about Jesus that most people in his day did not. Why did he call Jesus the Son of David? Where did he get that name from? It must have come to him through revelation. Jesus is the fulfillment of the covenant God made with David when He said his kingdom and throne would endure forever (see 2 Samuel 7:16). Jesus is the fulfillment of that covenant and the heir to David's throne, who will rule this world forever and ever.

Peter preached about this on the day of Pentecost. A major part of Peter's message was about David. He said that Jesus being raised from the dead fulfilled the promise God made. When the Jewish people heard it and understood, they ran to Peter asking what they should do. He told them to repent—which means to change thought patterns.

When Jesus heard someone calling Him the Son of David, He immediately stopped and told the people to bring the blind man to Him. Bartimaeus understood Jesus from a kingdom perspective and put a demand on Him, and He couldn't refuse the need of that person. That is why He healed blind Bartimaeus.

Free to Choose the Kingdom

There is nothing much for mankind outside of God's kingdom. Whatever we have outside of His kingdom is temporary and meaningless. God is committed to His kingdom, and He will move heaven and earth to help or to protect one of His sons who is doing His will. He will overrule any natural or spiritual laws, change any governments, or overthrow any emperors to see the calling of a son in His kingdom come to pass.

God will overthrow kingdoms and rebuke kings for His son's sake. He will even send a bird to feed a person who is doing His will, even in fear or in doubt. He will forgive and show mercy, even to a thousand generations, to those who are interested in His kingdom, who want to see His will accomplished on earth as it is in heaven. It means nothing to Him if you have been a member of a church or a particular denomination for many decades or even in ministry for any number of years. His priority is His kingdom.

God did not create the earth and put humans in it to eventually populate heaven. He never thought about such things, even in His wildest dreams. I am talking in human terms here. While He was on the earth, Jesus never asked even a single human if he or she wanted to go to heaven when they died.

Jesus did not come with an "earth-escaping-heaven-going" message; He came with a "bringing-heaven-to-earth" message. It is God's age-old plan of colonizing earth with heaven—He wanted earth to be an extension of heaven, His kingdom.

If mankind refuses to live in God's kingdom, then God is not responsible for the suffering they bring upon themselves or what the devil brings on mankind. That is what happened to Adam. He broke the boundary and went outside of God's kingdom, and ever since, mankind has been suffering because of that one man's transgression.

In His mercy, God decided to restore His kingdom back to us. That is why Jesus came with the message of the kingdom. He wanted all mankind back in His kingdom. The reason for each individual's existence is connected to His kingdom, and He has an assignment for each of them. He is committed to provide for and protect them.

That is why Jesus said that not even one little sparrow will fall and die without knowledge of the heavenly Father. Not a single hair falls from our heads to the ground without His knowledge. Then you may ask: why does He allow such terrible suffering upon humanity? The simple reason is because they are not living in His kingdom. They missed the blueprint.

The Bible stories are not fables—they are real history of the valiant things God's ambassadors did for His kingdom on earth. These ambassadors were not wishy-washy, Sunday-morning-only, prosperity-preaching deceivers. They gave their lives for one reason: so that by the time they died, God's kingdom would be extended another inch. They wanted God's will to be accomplished in one more area of life, even if they had to risk their own lives to see it happen.

That is what we read in the pages of the Bible, and it is the reason the Bible was written—so we can follow in their footsteps. It was not written for us to preach about it on a weekend. It was written as a manual for all kingdom citizens to follow.

What Is Real Freedom?

You can live in the most politically free country and not be free to fulfill your Father's kingdom assignment. In fact, the majority of people think that real freedom means being able to go where they want to go and do what they want to do. But that is not real freedom.

Real freedom is when a person is able to choose what God created him or her to do while he or she is on this planet. Doing whatever you want to do when you want to do it is not freedom—it is a deception. You are misusing your God-given free will and dishonoring the person who gave you that freedom. If everyone thought and did what they wanted to do when they wanted to do it, without being held responsible for their actions, most people would not even be alive.

Let's say I gave you a thousand dollars and told you to go and buy me ice cream. Then, because you are a free person, you took the money, squandered it, and never bought me the ice cream. What would I think of you? I wouldn't think very highly of someone who would do that.

That is not really freedom. The same principle applies to God, who gave us our lives and the ability to do a specific assignment for Him. But then we go and do whatever we want to do with those things. Get ready to face some accountability!

We were slaves to sin before we met Jesus. He bought us with a price, and we belonged to Him from that moment onward. You belong to the person who bought you, and your freedom was given to you at someone else's expense, so you are not free to do what you want to do; you can only do the will of the one who bought you. In this case, it is Jesus.

The good news is that Jesus sets people free. He bought them not so they would continue in any type of bondage or tyranny, but to do what they were created to do. Being able to walk in your calling brings joy and peace. That is why the Bible says that "if the Son makes you free, you shall be free indeed" (John 8:36).

When Jesus said this, the Jewish religious leaders began to murmur. They claimed they were Abraham's seed and were not in bondage to anyone. But that was a lie—they were in bondage in Egypt, and they were under the oppression of Rome even while they were saying these things to Jesus.

Furthermore, they were so bound to their religious system that they could not recognize their Messiah—even though He was walking and talking with them and standing right in front of them. That is what deception does to a person. Your freedom can stand right in front of your eyes and you can miss it!

If you can read a book like this and then go and read a fiction book next and pretend that nothing has happened to you, it is a sign of demonic deception—the same deception that the Jewish people in the first century were under. They cried out for the freedom of Barabbas and gave up their true King to be crucified. That is the sad state of the world we are living in today. People are being taught the wrong definition of freedom.

I had to close down churches and schools in order to obey my kingdom assignment. I was born and brought up in a Christian Pentecostal religion. I never heard a message about the kingdom of God until I was twenty-five years old—the most important subject to God and Jesus. I spent five years of my life in Bible schools, and yet there was not a single subject about the kingdom of God.

Another reason why needy people are not receiving the help they need is because the people who are supposed to be helping them are not walking in their callings. When a kingdom functions the way it is supposed to function, there will not be anyone with an unmet need.

That is what happened to the people of Israel in the Promised Land and also what happened in the early church. The Bible says that nobody had an unmet need. Now that is how the kingdom is supposed to work!

> Now the multitude of those who believed were of one heart and one soul; neither did anyone say that any of the things he possessed was his own, but they had all things in common. And with great power the apostles gave witness to the resurrection of the Lord Jesus. And great grace was upon them all. Nor was there anyone among them who lacked; for all who were possessors of lands or houses sold them, and brought the proceeds of the things that were sold, and laid *them* at the apostles' feet; and they distributed to each as anyone had need. (Acts 4:32–35)

Now that we are sure of our kingdom purpose, in the following chapters we are going to look into another important component of our blueprint, without which no one will fulfill his or her assignment in the kingdom.

CHAPTER 9

THE POWER OF KINGDOM IDENTITY

Every person at some point in their life has struggled with his or her identity. Feeling insecure about who we are, how we look, and what we can do or cannot do is a universal problem. Because of insecurity, many sabotage or shy away from what God has called them to do and live their lives in obscurity.

Many children of God cancel or give away their birthright and surrender their calling in the kingdom because of ignorance and insecurity. Others build their identity based on what they do or have. In this chapter, we will explore our true identity in the kingdom of God to bring security about who we are and to help us fulfill what He has called us to do by receiving its full benefits.

God Determines Our Identity

How does God see us? How does He want to relate with us? From the beginning of time, He wanted to relate with us as sons or children. Who was Adam? Was he a gardener? Was he a preacher? A businessman? Taking care of the garden was the work God gave Adam, but that was not his identity. Our identity is different from what we do. We don't see Adam preaching any sermons, either. What you do does not define who you are. Your name, job or work, or calling does not determine your identity in the kingdom of God.

In the kingdom, whose you are and where you came from (your source) determine your identity. If you ask Adam who He was, where he came from, and what his address was, he will say, "I am a son of God, created to protect and take care of this garden and this entire planet that my Father has given me. I came from God and I live in a country called the kingdom of God." The Bible says that Adam was the son of God. If you asked for his mailing address, it would look something like this:

Adam the Son of God (name)

1 Garden Road (street)

Eden (city), Kingdom of God (country)

Earth (planet) G27815 (postal code: Genesis 2:7, 8 and 15)

Your race, nationality, language, ethnicity, profession, color, and size do not determine your identity in the kingdom. Those could be part of the identity of where your body came from. But you are not your body.

God is the only One who is qualified to determine our identity because we came from Him. Adam was not Jewish, German, Indian, Chinese, African, or Caucasian. He was a human being created in the image and likeness of God. In the kingdom there is only one race—the human race.

Adam was not a Pentecostal, charismatic, Catholic, Baptist, or Lutheran. Jesus never called anyone a Pentecostal or charismatic. The first human, Adam, was a son of God, and the Last Adam is a Son of God as well. Whoever is born from Him and through Him bears the same image and likeness and are called the sons of God.

Sons Living Like Slaves

Your identity as sons is very important in the kingdom. Because of your assignment, the Father's inheritance and blessings flow to you based on your identity. You can be a son but live like a servant or a slave in your own father's house and not enjoy any blessings. That is why many of God's children are not enjoying the inheritance their Father gave to them.

One of the most profound and sad verses in the New Testament is what the father of the prodigal son told his older son. Though this son lived with his father and was entitled to everything his father owned, he never enjoyed any of the blessings, because his mindset was that of a slave. He did not know how to live like a son in his own father's house. We are going to look into that in detail shortly, because this happens to many believers.

Most believers live way below their potential and do not benefit from the blessings their Father has waiting for them. They are slaving their lives away and working so hard to provide for themselves, just trying to survive, while their Father owns the whole universe!

The Parable of Two Sons

To show us our identity and position in the kingdom, Jesus shared a powerful parable in Luke 15. The religious world calls it the parable of the prodigal son, but this parable is about two sons. Both sons are equally important in the story.

The parable begins by saying, "A certain man had two sons" (Luke 15:11). No specific qualifications or names were mentioned about these sons. Culturally, they both were future heirs. What qualified them to be sons? In the same train of thought, how did Adam become the son of God? What did he have to do to qualify to be a son of God? Nothing; it was his birthright.

In the parable, it does not say one son was more spiritual than the other. It does not indicate that one prayed every morning and the other did not and that was how they gained their sonship. Sonship is your birthright in the kingdom. It is not based on your performance or any specific qualifications. It comes by birth.

Their birth order is mentioned. The younger one asked his father for the portion of goods and the father gave him what was his. It is important to notice that the word *inheritance* is not used in these verses. An inheritance comes by maturity and by natural order. Before a father dies, he writes in the will what he would like to do with what he owns and to whom he wants it given. After his death, the children inherit whatever their father designated for them.

The younger son did not want to wait to *inherit*; he wanted his portion early because there was something happening inside of his heart that caused him to want to leave his home and father. We are going to find out what was happening in his heart.

The younger son sold everything the father gave, journeyed into a far country, and wasted all of his possessions. When he began to starve with hunger, he went to a citizen of that country to see if he would give him at least the pods that swine ate. But nobody gave him anything.

There he had a self-realization of who he was and what was happening in his father's house, so he decided to go back to his father and ask for his forgiveness to see if the father would receive him back as a servant.

At the same time, the older son was not doing any better. Though he was a son, he worked as a servant in his own house for payment.

The sad plight of both of these sons is that neither one of them functioned as sons or fulfilled the responsibility of their sonship. They never enjoyed the benefit of their sonship while living in their father's house. Something went tragically wrong in their relationship with their father. We will talk about that more in a minute.

Sadly, this happens to many in the kingdom these days. Though positionally they are sons, they are not benefiting from their sonship. They are slaving their lives away trying to please their Father. The more they try, the more impossible it seems.

When the prodigal son returned, the father threw a party for him. Instead of receiving him as a servant, the father decided to restore him to sonship. Then, when the older brother came in from the field after a long day of servitude, he heard all the singing and partying in his father's house. Other servants told him that his younger brother had returned and that his father had arranged a celebration. He became furious and refused go inside the house.

It is interesting to note the response of this older son. What made him so angry? Why wouldn't he accept his younger brother back? There was something going on in his heart, as well. He was having an identity crisis in his own heart and how he related with his father and his brother. This son believed that his father loved him based on what he did for him and how well he behaved. Since his younger brother ran away and wasted his father's possessions, according to him, the younger brother should not have been accepted back into the family.

Every other relationship we have is a reflection of our relationship with our heavenly Father. If our relationship with God is not in the right place, then we will have problems in our interpersonal relationships. If we do not believe God loves us, then we will not love ourselves. If we do not love ourselves, we cannot love anyone around us.

The concept of God is formed in a child's heart through their relationship with their parents, especially the father. The purpose of parenting is to model the heart and nature of God to our children, and then when they become mature, we are supposed to release them to their true Father in heaven. As they mature, they are supposed to transition from their earthly parents to their heavenly Father.

When children are little, they do the will of their parents. As they mature, they are supposed to be trained to do the will of their heavenly Father. That is why the enemy hates marriage and parenting and why these are screwed up in every culture. Instead of raising up sons and daughters who do the will of God, most people feel like orphans when they become adults and end up sleeping with pigs and eating their food. Once they become of age, they live their lives as if they have no father, never knowing their purpose and true identity.

This happens because of their upbringing and because they didn't transition into their relationship with their heavenly Father. Instead, they were taught religion. I know of parents who have children who are fifty years old, and they still will not release them to God or let go of their control. They keep holding onto them because of their own insecurity and unmet emotional needs.

This older son got up every morning to go to his father's field with the servants, working from morning until evening, maybe only receiving a basic wage for his labor. Though he was a son, he was living like a slave in his own father's house.

The reason this older son was slaving his life away was to please his father, thinking that one day he would notice his hard work and reward him with a goat to celebrate with his friends. Unfortunately, that day never came.

There are many children of God who are living like servants in the kingdom. When they see others are blessed, they become furious, jealous, or upset with God. They think God is not fair or just—that He blesses others while they are working hard for Him, trying to please Him with their good behavior, religious works, and rituals all these years, but never receive anything spectacular other than what they need to merely survive.

Wrong Perception of the Father

Now we have to ask: what caused this younger son to run away from his father's house? And what made the older brother go to work with the servants every day? This happened because of the wrong perception they had of their father.

The Bible does not say this father was mean or that he punished either of these sons. He did not treat them badly at any given time. He is pictured as the most loving and perfect father. The father in this parable represents our heavenly Father.

The problem with these two sons is that their identity was formed based on a wrong perception of their father. They did not recognize their father's heart, the reason for all the wealth he owned, or what he expected of them. They did not know how to function as sons in their father's kingdom.

As a result, the younger son ran away and squandered his father's possessions, while the older tried to earn it through hard work. The younger did not feel worthy, and the older one depended on his own works or performance by working hard in his father's field. The younger struggled with low self-esteem, and the older struggled with self-righteousness.

At least the younger son understood that he was an heir, and he had the right to own or use what his father had. He knew when his father died, he would receive his portion, but he wanted it early. That was why he went and asked his father for it.

The older was waiting for that perfect day—at some unknown time in the future when his father would call him and give him a little something. He was trying to prove to his father through his performance that he was worthy to receive some blessing, so he kept working harder and harder to prove that he was qualified to receive his wealth. But that day never came. The father was waiting for him to come to him as a son and ask for anything he wanted, while the son was waiting for the father.

Both sons misunderstood their father and his character. This is what the devil does to us—he misrepresents God's character, nature, and purpose, causing us to question His goodness. He wants us to believe that our Father is not good like He says He is.

If you are like the younger son and run away from the assignment your Father has for you, know that you can return anytime, and your Father will receive you back and throw a party for you. Don't live with the pigs anymore and eat their food. Come home; there is plenty at the table for you!

Though we are positionally sons (like the two sons in the parable), it is possible for us to live like slaves. Your blessings and inheritance in the kingdom are connected to your identity. If you do not position yourself rightly, you won't receive much. You will be slaving away like the older son in the parable, trying to make a living. Or you might run away like the younger son did.

> Now I say *that* the heir, as long as he is a child, does not differ at all from a slave, though he is master of all, but is under guardians and stewards until the time appointed by the father. Even so we, when we were children, were in bondage under the elements of the world. But when the fullness of the time had come, God sent forth His Son, born of a woman, born under the law, to redeem those who were under the law, that we might receive the adoption as sons.
>
> And because you are sons, God has sent forth the Spirit of His Son into your hearts, crying out, "Abba, Father!" Therefore you are no longer a slave but a son, and if a son, then an heir of God through Christ. (Galatians 4:1–7)

The verses above show us that it is possible for a son to live like a slave until he has matured in his understanding of identity. Until he reaches maturity, he is no better than a slave. Sadly, most people never reach that place of maturity.

That is what happened with the older son. He even confessed to his father that he had been working faithfully serving him and had never disobeyed his commandments not even to have a party with his friends.

He had served more faithfully than all the servants. Then he complained that after all these years of faithful serving, his father had never even given him even a skinny goat to enjoy with his friends (Luke 15:29).

His father might have owned thousands of sheep, cattle, fatted calves, and camels *and this son had the right to enjoy any of them at any time he wanted.* All the wealth of his father was at his disposal, but he did not know it. His father's reply is one of the most profound but sad verses in the New Testament.

His father said, "Son, you are always with me, and all that I have is yours" (Luke 15:31). That might be the most shocking thing this son ever heard from his father. All the sheep he had been taking care of all these years and all the fields and farms he was working for belonged to him—for him to enjoy.

All the fattened calves that he looked at and desired to eat one day were his the whole time. So why didn't he ever enjoy them? It was due to his false identity created by his immaturity, stemming from the wrong perception of his father.

The Origin of the Wrong Perception

In the book of Genesis, this is how the devil cast doubt on our Father's character and nature. The serpent told the woman, "For God knows that in the day you eat of it your eyes will be opened and you will be like God, knowing good and evil" (Genesis 3:5).

In other words, the serpent was saying, "See, God is hiding something from you. He is not as good as you think He is. He didn't tell you everything you need to know. He doesn't really want you to know who you are and what you can become. If He is really good, then He should have told you this."

That has been the enemy's method of operation from the beginning of time. He wants to misrepresent our Father and His character to us.

He wants us to question His nature and goodness, and then take life into our own hands and try to make it happen. If God is really good, then why is all this evil happening? If God really loves me, then why did He allow accidents, death, pain, or abuse? Why didn't He answer my prayer or meet my needs? Whatever the enemy uses in your life to cause you to question the goodness of God stems from a lie.

The goal is to twist your identity by twisting the nature and character of God. If our perception and relationship with God is not right, then our view of ourselves and our identity also will not be right. Your function in the kingdom is based on the understanding you have of your identity. Your identity is connected to the concept you have of God. If your identity is not right, then what you do and why you do it also won't be right or be done for the right reason.

This revelation will expose the lie that the devil has been using to deceive mankind, which is the primary weapon he uses to misrepresent our heavenly Father to us.

If God is good, then why don't most people believe it? If there is only one God, then why are there millions of gods and a myriad of religions? If there is only one Jesus and one gospel of the kingdom, then why are there so many different kinds of churches and denominations?

All of these came from a misunderstanding of God and misinterpretation of the Scriptures. God is the most misunderstood Person in the universe, and the message Jesus came to preach is the most misinterpreted message on the planet. Where and how did this misunderstanding begin?

This all began in Genesis chapter 3 when the serpent began to talk with the woman, Eve. He sowed seeds of doubt into man's heart about His nature, character, and intent. He made it sound like God was hiding or withholding something from us and that He knows something that He hasn't told us about.

> And he said to the woman, "Has God indeed said, 'You shall not eat of every tree of the garden'?"
>
> And the woman said to the serpent, "We may eat the fruit of the trees of the garden; but of the fruit of the tree which *is* in the midst of the garden, God has said, 'You shall not eat it, nor shall you touch it, lest you die.'"
>
> Then the serpent said to the woman, "You will not surely die. For God knows that in the day you eat of it your eyes will be opened, and you will be like God, knowing good and evil." (Genesis 3:1–5)

In these five verses, the serpent spoke lies, the root cause of all evil and destruction we see on the earth. Every religion, denomination, death, sin, curse, war, divorce, disease, and bad or evil thing stemmed from those verses. Whatever happened to the first man and woman happened to the rest of humanity. We inherited a wrong perception of God the Father through Adam, just like we inherited our sinful nature from him. That is the power of wrong information. What you know or you think you know determines the outlook of your life.

Ever since that time, mankind has struggled with this wrong perception of God. That is why most people do not want anything to do with God. They would rather worship a creature, snake, or even a dog than God Almighty. They do this out of ignorance of who God truly is.

These two sons had the same problem. They did not understand their father, in spite of having the most wonderful father. The Bible does not say anything negative about this father. He never scolded or punished their sons not even once. He was the perfect father, who is a picture of our heavenly Father.

The younger son decided to leave his father and family because he had a wrong perception of his father. He did not lack anything; he had plenty of food and had servants to take care of him and cook for him. All he had to do was manage his father's property and do what his father told him to do.

The Lie from the Serpent

The reason the prodigal son decided to run away stems back to the same lie that the serpent told Eve: "The Father is hiding something; He's not giving you everything you deserve. You won't become everything you can be if you stay in your Father's house—otherwise He would have told you everything."

This son thought he would not get to do the things he wanted if he stayed at home. He thought life was boring there. He ran away because of selfish ambition, stemming from that wrong perception. He wanted to do his own thing.

So what did the younger son decide to do? He decided to declare independence from the father and his kingdom, collect his wealth and possessions, and live to do his own will instead of the father's. That has been the game plan of the devil from the beginning. Unfortunately, most of humanity has fallen prey to this ploy. They are not doing their Father's will; they are trying to survive on their own, trying to become like God in their own strength.

Adam went through the same experience. Why would he rebel against God? Why would he disobey his Father? The Father did no evil to him. It was for the same reason. The enemy convinced him that what God gave and told him so far was not good enough or complete and that there had to be more.

This is the same thing the enemy tells people today. So people seek this special knowledge because they think there is some teaching out there that will qualify them and make them like God. New Age teachings and Gnosticism are products of seeking this "special" knowledge apart from God.

God was not hiding or withholding anything from them. That is what the enemy made it sound like when he said, "For God knows that in the day you eat of it your eyes will be opened, and you will be like God, knowing good and evil" (Genesis 3:5). Every religion stemmed from that one single lie of the serpent—that you have to do something apart from God and what He has given you in order to become or to receive something from Him.

Already Qualified

Whatever belongs to the Father already belongs to us. He did not withhold anything from us. That is what this father told the older son when he said, "Son, you are always with me, and all that I have is yours" (Luke 15:31). Let's not disqualify ourselves from being a son of God by going after the things of this world and titles.

Adam did not have to do anything to qualify to become a son of God. It came by birth; the kingdom was given to him. He didn't work for the garden; he didn't have to earn it. It was a gift from the father to his son. This is the same way it works in the kingdom of God in the New Testament. The kingdom is a gift from the Father to His children. That is why He said, "Do not fear, little flock, for it is your Father's good pleasure to give you the kingdom" (Luke 12:32). He did not say we have to earn it, but that we receive it as a gift.

We do not need to shout, scream, or take it by force; it has been made available to us by our Father. All we have to do is to receive it. Sonship is a gift from the Father. The moment we try to add any personal merits to it, we disqualify ourselves from receiving the fatted calf.

It was the same for Adam; he did not have to do anything to become a son of God. He was not required to perform any rituals prior to meeting with his Father. All he had to do was to show up. God didn't do anything evil, say anything mean, or withhold anything from him. He gave Adam the entire planet and access to heaven and he still misunderstood God, thinking He was not good enough, all because of the influence of the devil.

Adam and Eve originally rebelled against God because they became convinced that God was not good enough, what He gave them was not sufficient enough, and He did not tell them everything He should have told them. They believed that if He were good enough, He wouldn't withhold the fruit of the tree of the knowledge of good and evil, which is what the serpent portrayed through his cunning words.

The serpent basically said, "God knows something that He hasn't told you about. He's hiding something you should know. If God told you everything you need to know, then you wouldn't be like this—you would be like God." What they failed to realize is that they were already like God and that He did not hide anything from them.

They could have asked Him for or about anything, and He would have given it to them or told them. He gave the entire planet to them and gave them free access to heaven anytime. He met with them personally every day. What more could He have done?

What the devil wanted was for mankind to declare independence from God and His kingdom and try to become like Him on their own by their personal efforts or religious works. The enemy knew that outside of our relationship with God, mankind can never achieve the goal of becoming like Him. He wanted to throw us into a perpetual delusion and misery of trying to become like God. This is the root of humanism and all religion.

It is same in the New Testament. Jesus gave us the whole kingdom, died for us, forgave all of our sins, made us righteous, and gave us access to His throne room 24/7. He promised to be with us until the end of the age. He gave us sonship, filled us with His Spirit, gave us access to heaven, seated us in Him in the heavenly places, and blessed us with all spiritual blessings but we still feel like God didn't do a good enough job for us!

On top of all of that, He gave us His only begotten Son so we can have salvation by grace, and He gave us the jurisdiction of the entire earth. Despite all of this, most of us are still living like orphans. The question is why? It is because of the wrong perception of the Father and His character.

Every time Christians come together, they start singing, expecting God to "show up," when in reality He has been living in them all along—He is already there. The religious spirit has deceived the masses, keeping them stuck in this perpetual delusion, never getting anywhere with their rituals.

We are trying harder, singing longer and louder, praying and sweating down to our underpants trying to please God, thinking if we just hit the "perfect note" in our music, one of these days He might come down and do something for us. We inherited this lie from our forefather Adam that originated all the way back in the book of Genesis.

TWO KINDS OF DEATH

Remember God told Adam that the day he ate from the tree of the knowledge of good and evil, he would die. God was not talking about physical death, but spiritual death—the death of his sonship. This meant that the day he ate from that tree, Adam would lose his sonship and the ability to relate to God as his Father. Man would lose the spirit of sonship. God calls it *death*.

The moment man puts his trust in anything outside of God's grace, love, and righteousness in order to be accepted by Him, he falls short of his position as a son in the kingdom.

When we are not functioning in the position of sonship in the kingdom, to God we are considered dead. He will not receive any benefit from us occupying space on earth and using its resources, and we will not be fulfilling the purpose He sent us here to do. As a result, we will not receive any blessings He has in store for us.

When the prodigal son came back, his father said the same thing: "For this my son was dead and is alive again" (Luke 15:24). He was not talking about a physical death. Physically he was alive, but he was not fulfilling his sonship in his house.

The father was talking about the death of sonship. When the prodigal son was away, he was not living as a son—he was living as a slave. When he returned home, his sonship was restored, and he came *alive*. When we are doing our own thing instead of the will of our Father, we are dead in our sonship and will not receive any benefits from our Father's house.

This son knew that the servants in his father's house would eat and have plenty of leftovers. But when he was away, he was starving and living with the pigs. His provision was not with the pigs; it was only found when he was at home in his father's house. When we embrace our sonship and live in our Father's house, doing His will, it is His responsibility to take care of us.

The serpent told the woman that if she ate from the tree of knowledge of good and evil, she would not die. The devil was talking about physical death—the second kind of death. They did not die physically right after they ate from that tree. He was deceiving them to kill their sonship so that he could steal their birthright to rule the earth. Once mankind's sonship in the kingdom is lost, he is equal to a dead person.

Sonship in the kingdom is what gives us the right to do anything on the earth. The devil stole our birthright as God's children, giving it to his children to rule and to reign on the earth. There are two kinds of seeds on this earth: the righteous seed and the seed of the wicked one.

Both the Old and New Testaments talk about two kinds of seeds. It began in Genesis when God declared that the seed of woman would crush the head of the serpent and He will put enmity between her seed and his seed. Ever since that time, there have been two kinds of humans on this planet.

The seed of the wicked do the will of their father, the devil. The seed of the righteous are supposed to do the will of their Father in heaven. Unfortunately, the majority of the righteous seed have been deceived by the devil, and by the spirit of survival they serve the kingdom of darkness for their livelihood. They do not benefit from the kingdom of their Father.

No one taught them about their sonship in the kingdom and their inheritance. Many are living in hunger and lack, which is prompting them to want to escape this planet. What is ironic is that they are longing to be with their Father in His kingdom. They misunderstand this as going to heaven when they die.

We were misinformed about the Father's house and where it is located. We were taught that it is located in somewhere in heaven, and after we die, we will go and inherit our mansions. But that is not what the Bible says.

Death of Sonship

In Genesis, when God instructed Adam and Eve not to eat from the tree of the knowledge of good and evil, it was for their protection. He didn't say it to hide something from them; He didn't want them to die, and He wasn't talking about physical death here.

God was talking about a different kind of death. He was talking about their separation from Him—the *death* of their sonship in His kingdom. When you lose your sonship or you start to function outside of sonship in the kingdom, God calls it *death*. When we are not fulfilling our responsibilities as sons in His kingdom, we are considered to be dead, meaning we are not useful to the Father anymore.

The moment Adam and Eve ate the fruit, they lost the ability to relate with God as their Father. They lost the Spirit of sonship. Regaining our sonship in the kingdom in our Father's house is called coming alive again or being born again.

In light of this, what the father said of his younger son in this parable is one of the most profound statements about our identity as sons in the kingdom of our Father. This father said, "For this my son was dead and is alive again; he was lost and is found" (Luke 15:24).

Only when we regain our sonship does God consider us to be *alive* in His kingdom. That is why I do not support the idea of leadership. You can be a great leader and still miss your sonship. God does not recognize leaders; He only recognizes sons in His kingdom. People spend a lot of money to be trained as leaders because it looks attractive to them in the natural. They get nothing from their Father's kingdom.

Two Viruses Deadlier Than COVID-19

We have already covered the fact that the reason the two sons behaved the way they did in the story of the prodigal son stemmed from their wrong perception of their father. So one ran away, and the other worked like a slave.

Two opposing perceptions were birthed from the lies the enemy told Adam and Eve. I call them *deadly viruses*. These viruses are deadlier than COVID-19 and have been killing many people. One perception is that *God is not good enough*. The other perception is legalism, which says that what *God did and gave is not enough,* and that you have to work to please God or to earn something from Him through good works. It says you have to do something to get something from God.

Religion causes us to believe that in order to please God, we have to do something. We get into a perpetual mode of striving to earn something from Him and trying to please Him, but we never reach the goal. Everyone who has ever been born inherited one of those perceptions, and we are all victims of one of these lies.

Every evil, religion, philosophy, and "-ism" originated from the five verses in Genesis 3, when the serpent questioned what God said. This is the beginning of every type of evil—questioning the boundaries God has set forth. Ever since that time, mankind has been questioning or pushing every healthy limit or boundary God has set forth in His Word.

People began to question God's authority in every area of life. Feminism came out of Genesis 3. The serpent talked to Eve instead of Adam and inspired her to take the lead. God did not bring her to the garden to lead Adam in anything. She was brought as a companion to Adam. She was supposed to be by his side, helping him do what he could not do—not listening to the serpent and doing things contrary to what God said and influencing Adam to do the same.

People have removed the boundaries God has put on almost every sphere of life. In family, sex/gender, raising children, government, education, and more, people have removed God and His boundaries and standards, establishing their own wills and agendas instead. They thought they were trying to make life better, trying to be smarter; instead, they destroyed it and continue to destroy it today.

Every religion came out of those five verses; humanism, communism, Gnosticism, and worship of creatures rather than the Creator. Disorder in marriage and family life, rebellion, sin, independence, individualism, gender confusion, the curse, sickness—everything came to this planet because and through what the serpent told the woman and because she believed what it said.

The devil wanted mankind to operate independently, apart from God, to become gods on their own and remove God from everything on earth. This is his ultimate plan. We were created like God, but now the devil wants us to try to *become* like God by doing works or rituals that God told us not to do. The devil wanted us to believe we can become like God by knowing good and evil. But we do not become like God by knowing good and evil; that is trying to attain spirituality by personal striving, discipline, or achievement.

This mentality is the foundation of many religions today. People are trying to attain a state of mind, spirituality, or a condition in themselves through meditation or various kinds of disciplines or rituals, repeating some kind of prayers, habits, or by personal afflictions. They afflict their bodies to attain something in the spirit, but they will never attain the likeness and image of God that way. We do not need to do anything to become like God—we were created like Him. It came as part of our birthright.

When you are affected by a virus, you will have certain symptoms. If you are affected by the virus of "God is not good enough," here are the symptoms that may manifest in your life:

- You will run away from your father's house—selfishness.
- You will have nothing to do with God or His kingdom.
- The enemy will steal and use what belongs to you to build his kingdom.
- You will waste your resources on physical pleasures and parties.
- You will not believe that God really loves you, so you will go looking for love from other people and other things.
- You will develop an orphan heart.
- You will have low self-esteem and a low opinion of yourself. You will end up sleeping with the pigs, eating and drinking things that you shouldn't.
- You will seek the acceptance and approval of others.

One good thing about this virus is that there is a potential for this person to return to his or her Father's house, and to be restored and receive the righteousness of God.

If you are infected by the second virus of "What God did is not good enough," these symptoms may manifest in your life:

- You will depend on your works to please God and be accepted by Him.
- You will become a perfectionist.
- You will be critical of yourself and others, and will not be able to truly love others.
- You will be committed to your own hurt (workaholic).
- You will be very legalistic and rules-oriented, living to keep the rules and obey them.
- You will not enjoy anything in life, because there is always more to do.
- You will be very judgmental of others and their weaknesses and have difficulty forgiving others.
- You will always work hard, but not achieve anything.
- You will not be able to receive the righteousness of God.
- It will be hard to repent and you will not recognize your own weaknesses.
- You will not achieve God's best; you will end up a *human doing* instead of a *human being*.
- You will not be able to receive the righteousness of God unless you are delivered from the religious spirit.

With the fall, man lost his position, birthright, and relationship with God, and the wrong perception of God, himself, and the world entered mankind. To change those wrong perceptions and to return to our original assignment, mandates, birthright, and position, God wants us to repent. That is why when Jesus came, the first word that came out of His mouth was *repent*. It means to change the way we think—to change the wrong perception we have about our Father, His kingdom, and why He put us on this planet. We need to change our thinking and return to His kingdom.

Instead, we built religions and denominations out of the word *repentance*. As a result, instead of life getting better, we created more wrong perceptions of God. People are more confused about God today than ever before.

CHAPTER 10

THREE LAYERS OF REVELATION HIDDEN IN THE PARABLE

There are three layers of kingdom mysteries that are hidden in the parable of the two sons. There might be more, but for the purpose of this book, I would like to mention only three.

Jesus shared this parable for a specific reason. Each one of our lives is a picture, or a reflection, of one of these sons. Before we are settled in our kingdom identity as sons, all of us will behave like one of them. We are going to look a little deeper to see what the Holy Spirit wants to show us from the lives of these sons.

There are three layers of revelation hidden in this parable. Let's see what they are.

The Two Sons Represent Two Races of People on Earth

God created only one race—the human race. Because the first man disobeyed and rebelled against God and His purpose, He chose one man and created a nation out of him. That man was Abraham. From him came the Jewish race, and God wanted to share His light and plan to the rest of the world through them.

The Bible talks about two races: Gentiles and Jews. We are all originally God's children; we all came from Adam. But because of the wrong perception of God that was instigated by demonic influence, people misunderstood God the Father. As a result, the first son, Adam, committed treason. Consequently, everyone born after him inherited a wrong perception of God.

There came a separation between Jews and the rest of mankind, which came to be known as Gentiles. Jewish people, the nation of Israel, were God's firstborn (Exodus 4:22). The older son in this parable represents the Jewish people, and younger son represents the Gentiles.

Though the Gentiles walked away from their Father, later, they returned to Him and restored their sonship in the kingdom. Jewish people depended on their own righteousness through the law, or works, and did not obtain righteousness.

Though they are the heirs of everything, they did not obtain the righteousness of God because they depended on their own works. Though God called them to be blessings to the entire world, they did not want to share their blessings. They were supposed to be showing the Gentiles the heart of their Father and the way to the Father. They failed miserably in their mission.

The responsibility of a firstborn or older brother is to be a model and example to the younger ones. Instead, they rejected the Gentiles and hated them. They were not willing to accept them as part of the family. In their sight, the Gentiles did not qualify to be part of the family because they didn't look and smell like them. Remember when Isaac was blind and he was trying to smell Esau before he blessed him to make sure it was really him?

Because the older brother did not do his job, the younger brother also inherited a wrong perception of God and did not want to serve or do the will of his father. So he decided to take his father's goods and run away.

One of the reasons this younger son decided to run away from his father's home is because of how his older brother treated him. This older son played a spiritual supremacy or superiority over his younger brother, looking down on him instead of mentoring him. That created a wrong perception in his heart about life and his father.

It is the same in the kingdom. The Jewish people looked down on the Gentiles, and as a result, the Gentiles rebelled against God and ran away from His kingdom with His goods. They have been living as strangers in a foreign land all these years, eating pigs' food and serving foreign gods. They are working hard, but never have enough. Inside, they are miserable, because they do not feel fulfilled.

The Gentiles worshiped and served all kinds of demons and false gods. They did not understand the true heart of God and His plan for the earth and mankind. They thought He was not good enough—that He kills, destroys, and punishes people and nations and they did not want to serve such a mean god. So they made their own gods, and they have been worshiping them ever since.

The Jewish people are trying to look more religious and obey the Old Covenant, not realizing that covenant was done away with once and for all on the cross. They are also trying to recruit the Gentiles to join their Jewish sect to look religious like they do. I have not yet seen one religious person who walks in the power of God. They have the "look," but they miss out on sonship and live like orphans.

Remember, God wanted Abraham to be a blessing to all the families of the earth, not just the Jewish race. He wanted the Jewish people to take the message of salvation through Jehovah to the ends of the earth. But they were not willing to share. Then when Jesus came, He was sent to the lost sheep of Israel. He wanted to restore them to their original intent. But they rejected Him again and His kingdom assignment. God had to take the message and the kingdom from them and give it to another nation instead (Matthew 21:43).

By the grace of God, the younger son (the Gentiles) decided to return to his father's house. The father was happy to have him back. He restored his sonship and arranged a big party for him. The older brother became so angry when he heard of it. He could not accept the favor his father extended to his younger brother. To him, this younger brother was not qualified anymore. He wasn't righteous or holy enough.

The older brother considered himself holier and more righteous than the younger brother because of his faithful servitude to the father. He thought he was serving his father, but in truth, he was doing his own will not the father's will. He was serving himself. His father never required him to go to the field and work with his servants. That is just what he thought his father wanted him to do. See what the wrong perception of God will do to people and their lives?

That is what happened to the Jewish people when Jesus came. They thought they were serving God by trying to keep all the laws of Moses. They thought they were doing God some favor. Every time Jesus tried to talk to them, they quoted scriptures to Him. Can you imagine trying to quote Scriptures to God? The very Word was walking in front of them and talking with them, but they did not recognize Him. They were quoting lines from the book to the Author who wrote it!

That is what a religious spirit will do to people. It will deceive them and cause them to serve the devil, and then convince them that they are serving God. They will quote verses from the Bible without knowing what the Scriptures really mean. How can a person believe they are serving God and at the same time fight against God and His very purpose? That is the power of deception. Anyone who opposes the kingdom of God and the gospel of the kingdom is deceived by the religious spirit. They just do not realize it.

Do you know how many people waste their lives doing their own will, but inside they think they are trying to please their Father or doing Him a favor? That is the deception of the religious spirit. Since they go to church for two hours on a Sunday, they think they are free to do whatever they want to do the rest of the week.

These two sons did not take the time to ask their father what he wanted them to do or what his will for their lives was. They did not ask what the purpose was for all the wealth their father owned. They were operating from a preconceived notion about the nature, character, and the expectations of their father that were totally false.

The Apostle Paul talks about this (Jews and Gentiles) in his epistle to the Romans:

> What shall we say then? That Gentiles, who did not pursue righteousness, have attained to righteousness, even the righteousness of faith; but Israel, pursuing the law of righteousness, has not attained to the law of righteousness. Why? Because *they did* not *seek it* by faith, but as it were, by the works of the law. For they stumbled at that stumbling stone. (Romans 9:30–32)

This older brother became angry at his father and his brother when he saw that his younger brother was accepted back into the family. Paul talks about it in Romans 10:19:

> I will provoke you to jealousy by *those who* are not a nation, I will move you to anger by a foolish nation.

When God extended His mercy and grace to the Gentiles, the Jewish people were not happy. They further rebelled against Him. Again, he talks about the Gentiles in Romans 9:25–26:

> I will call them My people, who were not My people, and her beloved, who was not beloved. And it shall come to pass in the place where it was said to them, "You *are* not My people." There they shall be called sons of the living God.

The older son depended on his own works (self-righteousness) to receive blessings from his father. But he did not receive any more than what was needed for mere survival. Do you know how many Christians live every day on mere survival?

The younger son thought his father was mean and not good enough, and that if he stayed in his father's house, he wouldn't have everything he could have or wouldn't have the freedom to do what he wanted with his life. So he decided to run away. This is what happened to the Jews and the Gentiles. They both missed God because of the wrong perception they had of Him.

The Two Sons Represent the Entire Human Race

These two sons represent the entire human race—every person who was ever born. All religions and denominations were birthed out of the wrong perception of God. Because people thought God was not good enough, they started other religions and began to worship false gods.

The older son could not accept his younger brother. To him, his brother was lost and could never be restored. He felt that even if he came back, his father should not accept him back into the house. Self-righteous people are unable to show mercy; they won't show mercy to themselves and are hard on themselves, and they will be hard on others, too.

It is hard for humans to admit total depravity. They will try to find some kind of merit, either based on their race, heredity, education, skills, what their grandparents did, and more. That is what the Jewish people told Jesus every time He tried to reach out to them; they kept boasting about their history.

This older son could not even accept his brother. When he was talking to his father, he said, "As soon as this son of yours came." Self-righteous people have a hard time accepting others. They think of themselves as superior and nobody is as good as they are. They talk and treat others as if everybody else is beneath them.

Then this older son passed a judgment on his brother, saying he had "devoured your livelihood with harlots." That was the opinion he had of his brother. Self-righteous people are judgmental and critical of others. They will keep passing judgment on people based on their pasts. Because of this, the older brother disqualified himself from receiving anything from his father, even though his father owned everything.

Self-righteous people look at people based on their works, especially what they did in the past. The real reason this older son worked for his father was not because he cared about his father or his property, but because he was hoping that someday he would receive the fatted calf. That was the motivation behind his hard labor; he wanted to qualify himself.

Some of us belong in the older-son category, depending on our own works, trying to please God or to receive something from Him as reward for our good behavior. The other group belongs to the younger-son category, who have no merits of their own to claim and fall at the mercy of God, expressing their utter helplessness and hopelessness. They receive righteousness by faith because of what their Father has done for them.

Jesus shared another parable about two men who went to pray:

> Also He spoke this parable to some who trusted in themselves that they were righteous, and despised others: "Two men went up to the temple to pray, one a Pharisee and the other a tax collector. The Pharisee stood and prayed thus with himself, 'God, I thank You that I am not like other men—extortioners, unjust, adulterers, or even as this tax collector. I fast twice a week; I give tithes of all that I possess.' And the tax

collector, standing afar off, would not so much as raise *his* eyes to heaven, but beat his breast, saying, 'God, be merciful to me a sinner!' I tell you, this man went down to his house justified *rather* than the other; for everyone who exalts himself will be humbled, and he who humbles himself will be exalted." (Luke 18:9–14)

The Two Sons Represent the Two Covenants

This one parable contains the entire Old and New Covenant reality. Jesus did not come to authorize the old, but to fulfill and remove it. He established a New Covenant, but many people are still stuck in the Old Covenant. They keep going back to Moses to find another trophy to attach to the list of their self-righteous acts, telling God why He should bless them with a fatted calf. But they never receive one—not even a skinny goat.

The older son represents the Old Covenant, and the younger son represents the New Covenant. The Old Covenant was based on works: if you do good, you will be accepted by God, and when you disobey, you will be punished or cursed.

In the New Covenant, God accepts a person not based on his or her works, but rather based on the finished work on the cross through Jesus Christ and the person's faith in it. When the younger son came back, his father did not take into consideration anything he did while he was gone from his house. This son may have committed some gross sins that he would be ashamed of telling to anyone else.

The father did not ask him about any of that; instead, he ordered the servants to bring the best robe to be put on him. That means the father forgave his son of everything he did even before he arrived. That is what our Father in heaven did for us through Jesus. He forgave the sins of the whole world when Jesus died on the cross. He judged our sins on the cross, and the punishment that was due unto us fell on Jesus.

That is why the Bible says that when we were enemies of God, He reconciled us with Him through Jesus (Romans 5:10). Before we arrived in the kingdom, God already forgave all of our sins two thousand years ago. We come in and acknowledge it by faith and receive back our rightful positions of sonship in His kingdom. Many people stay at the door, thinking they are not worthy or qualified to come in. They are stuck in their self-righteousness or their ignorance of what their Father has done for them.

Others go digging for the dead bones of their forefathers all the way back to Adam, trying to make up for all the sins and asking God for forgiveness. They do not realize that those sins were all wiped clean by the blood of Jesus. We need to acknowledge and appropriate it by faith.

They do not enter the kingdom of their father or their sonship, and keep wandering around the house of their own Father, laboring like a slave and feeling angry at their Father for blessing those who didn't deserve it. They cry and keep on repenting of the same sins, but they never really feel forgiven. They act as though they have to do more for God to forgive them, as though what Jesus did on the cross is not good enough.

Because people wrongly interpreted what God is expecting from mankind in the Scriptures, they began to focus on different truths of the Bible, and thus birthed all these different denominations. They all say that God requires something different from humans, and that we have to perform to make God happy or to please Him so He will give us a fatted calf at some point. A "fatted calf" represents any blessing or favor we hope to receive from God.

The sad truth is that we became like one of these sons and missed the blessing, when all that was required of us was to live like sons in His family or kingdom and manage His property. Lord help us!

Many sons of God are trying or working so hard to earn what already belonged to them. They don't know what qualifies them to receive what their Father has stored up for them. That's what we are going to look into in the next chapter.

CHAPTER 11

THE POWER OF KINGDOM BIRTHRIGHT

Have you ever wondered why Christians feel as though they do not belong on the earth or why most Christians are misinformed of their purpose? Why do the majority of believers struggle to find resources to fulfill what they are called to do? Why it is so hard for Christians to have unity among themselves? Other religious groups don't have a problem with unity. There is a specific reason for all of these problems.

We have a very limited understanding about what really happened to Adam and the rest of mankind when he committed sin. The general belief is that Adam lost heaven when He disobeyed God, and Jesus came to take us all back to heaven. That is not what the Bible teaches.

Very few people understand the magnitude of the loss mankind experienced with the fall of the first man, Adam. In this chapter, we are going to explore what happened to Adam and Eve and why God had to send another Adam to die in our place.

Stealing the Birthright

We as Christians are the ones who preach and teach about love and unity, but there are more divisions among us than among any other religious group! There is a specific reason for this, and it all began with the fall of Adam. If you put two or more believers together, soon they will find something they cannot agree on, and someone will get offended and leave. This does not happen very much with other religious groups. People think revival will unite the body of Christ. But there have been many revivals all throughout history, and we still are divided! Until we study, discover, and rectify the issue at the root, nothing will change for the better.

So what was the serpent really after when he tried to deceive Adam and Eve? Was he trying to steal the garden? Was he attempting to send them to hell? Was he trying to hurt them physically with sickness and curses? Was he trying to steal the gold and precious stones from the garden? What would he get personally out of all of these?

The serpent was after something specific. He knew what gave Adam and Eve the right to do what they did, to be who they were, and to have what they had. That is what he was after. He knew that if he could steal that right from them, then he could use it do what they were created to do and then take ownership of what was given to them by their Father.

The devil became a homeless, unemployed cherub due to his rebellion and fall and was looking to gain an opportunity to reestablish his kingdom on the earth. In order to do that, he had to receive the right, or permission. Mankind was the only species authorized by God to rule on the earth. His goal was to obtain it from mankind through deception.

It was Adam's birthright that gave him the right to do what he was doing and to have what he had—his birthright as a son in his Father's kingdom. Once he lost the birthright, he was as good as dead. A legal transaction took place between Adam and the serpent through the deception and the fall, which is how Adam lost his right to rule the earth, and how the serpent and his seed obtained it illegally.

What the enemy stole from Adam was his birthright. When a person loses his or her birthright, he or she loses every other right to do anything in a country. Rulership over the earth was part of Adam's birthright. That is why believers all over the world feel as though they don't belong on the earth because they have been operating without their kingdom birthright.

The enemy stole it from us and used it to build his kingdom and to empower his seed to do things on the earth. That is why ungodly people prosper while believers look at them with envy. They do all the charismatic gymnastics and still don't prosper, and then they wonder what is going on in their lives.

The reason why the majority of believers don't know what they are supposed to do with their lives and don't prosper is because their birthright have been stolen by the enemy and they don't even realize it! They think they're just waiting to disappear from the earth and that God doesn't want them to do anything significant. But their spirit man is crying out to see the purpose that they were sent to earth begin to manifest in their lives.

Right after Adam sinned, he felt as though he did not belong in the garden or on the earth anymore. He was removed from the garden, and then he couldn't find the things he needed for his survival. He couldn't exercise the rights he had before because he lost them. He felt like an outcast. Once a person loses his or her birthright, they lose all other rights that come with it. They won't receive any benefits from the country of their citizenship, and they have no right to do anything legal.

Once Adam lost his birthright, he felt like an orphan. When he lost the Spirit of sonship, an orphan spirit began to operate in him. He was afraid to face God. I call this the Orphan Heart Syndrome (OHS). When a person is affected by an orphan spirit or heart, these are the symptoms he or she will experience in their lives emotionally:

- I'm not good enough
- I don't belong here
- I have to make it happen (survival)

- Nobody loves me, or everybody is against me
- I can't do anything right
- I don't have what it takes
- Something is wrong with me
- Insecurity or superiority (based on how we look, the color of our skin, nationality, or even gender)

When a bunch of people who are orphan-hearted come together, they won't be able to accept each other because they don't feel accepted or loved within themselves. Instead, they will start looking for approval from others. When their opinions are not received, they feel rejected or offended. They will react by doing and saying offensive things without realizing it. As a result, they will pick up their bags and go and start their own ministries or withdraw into their caves. That is one of the main reasons there isn't unity among the body of Christ. The majority of us are living with orphan hearts or spirits.

When you marry a person who has an orphan heart, and he or she is not affirmed as a person, not validated in their identity, and not approved as a person, they will begin to demand approval, appreciation, and acceptance. When they don't receive it, they will project their problem onto their spouse. Their marriage will become a battlefield. They are oversensitive, emotionally needy, and will become extremely stubborn.

Restoration of the Birthright

The first thing God restores to us when we come into the kingdom is our birthright. That is why the Bible says, "But as many as received Him, to them He gave the right to become children of God, to those who believe in His name" (John 1:12).

Though God gave us our birthright, many people don't grow to become matured sons of God. They remain like young children while the enemy and the wicked ones continue to use their birthright to rule the earth and prosper in what they do. The reason they do not mature is because they do not receive the spiritual food they require.

Instead of discovering, activating, and functioning in their birthright, believers are further deceived and chase things like leadership and success, thinking that will qualify them to do what God created them to do. In the end, they just become more frustrated and feel hopeless.

It's time for the sons of God all over the world to rise up and receive back their birthright, and then cancel every illegal birthright the enemy has been using to build his kingdom. Whatever the enemy and the wicked have been doing, they are doing it illegally. They have no right to do anything! But nothing will change for the better until the sons of God rise up and start to exercise their birthright.

If you are forty or fifty years old and still have no clarity on what you are supposed to do with your life, know that your birthright has been stolen from you. Or, if you are struggling to find the resources to fulfill your kingdom assignment, know that your birthright and your inheritance in the kingdom have not been released yet.

If you have tried everything and nothing is working out or prospering yet, know that the problem is with your birthright. If you received prophetic words and promises and nothing has come to pass yet, know that the problem lies with your birthright. Many are waiting for that perfect day when things will just start happening. Your waiting season is over. It's time to take back what the enemy stole from you. It doesn't matter how long you have been a Christian or a church member.

Consequences of Losing Birthright

When a child is born into a family, that child is not required to do anything to receive food, care, and nourishment from its parents. That child doesn't need to clean anything or even thank them, because it can't. That is the way it is in the kingdom. When you are born into the kingdom of God, it is your Father's responsibility to provide for and take care of you.

When you become an adult, the Father uses your assignment in His kingdom to continue to provide for you. This process will go on until your last breath. You are not your own; you belong to a King and His kingdom.

Adam was the first human, so whatever happened to him happened to the rest of humanity. When Adam sinned, we were in him. Whatever God told Adam is true for all humanity. Whatever He gave him belongs to the rest of humanity. Whatever Adam did or did not do affects the rest of mankind. Why? He was the prototype; we all came from him. This is the foundational truth of all biblical doctrine.

When Adam lost the birthright, the rest of mankind lost it with him. When he lost the right to rule this planet, the rest of humanity lost the right. That is why Christians have a hard time accepting the fact that God created them to rule the earth because their birthright have not been restored yet.

If you tell an individual who lost his birthright about rulership, he can't accept it because it doesn't make any sense to him. He is just struggling to survive and to make a living, and you come along and tell him that he is supposed to be ruling and reigning. He will mock you!

I did not understand this for a long time. I tried to convince believers through the scriptures, books and through our Kingdom School courses that they were created by God to rule this planet. It didn't make any sense to them at first. Instead, they were looking for the next new song that was coming out, for a new job they were going to apply for, or for another prophetic word about their futures. They were afraid for their survival. That's when the Lord began to point out to me saying the issue is with their birthright.

Birthright is the foundation on which the rest of our lives are built. When there is no birthright, there is no foundation. This is why believers are waiting to fly away; they are so tired of life and feeling helpless because they are not able to do much on earth. They can't impact their nations and are tired of sitting and watching what the enemy and his seed are doing in their communities.

Here are some of the things Adam lost when he lost his birthright:

- His sonship
- His Father
- The kingdom of God/the garden
- Provision
- Access to heaven
- The right to rule the earth

By losing the birthright, Adam lost all of his other rights, his inheritance, and his assignment—he lost the right to do anything on the earth. The Lord gave Adam everything mentioned above as part of his birthright. It was not because he did anything good or obeyed certain commandments; they were given to him the moment he was created.

First and Last Adam

When Adam sinned against God, we were in him. When Adam fell, we fell with him. Whatever happened to the first man happened to the rest of humanity. When Eve ate from the tree first, nothing happened to her or Adam yet; it wasn't until Adam took his bite that they both fell. He was the first man to whom God gave the right to rule. Eve was taken out of Adam; he was her source.

Every defect, weakness, sin nature, evil, death, loss of sonship, sickness—everything negative we experience in this life—we inherited from the first Adam. The good news is that this is not the end of the story. What you received from the first Adam is not the final report.

Because of God's great love for us and His great mercy toward us, He decided to send another Adam to the earth. Then He gave us another opportunity to become born again through this Adam, whom the Bible calls the last Adam (1 Corinthians 15:45).

We received everything evil from the first Adam through our natural birth; likewise, through our spiritual birth, we receive everything that is in the last Adam. We have a choice to make: whether to remain in the first Adam or in the last Adam.

Jesus Christ, the Son of the living God, is the last Adam. To whoever receives Him and believes in His name, the first thing God restores is his or her birthright in the kingdom.

But as many as received Him, to them He gave the right to become children of God, to those who believe in His name. (John 1:12)

But instead of teaching a new believer about his or her birthright and sonship in the kingdom, we've taught them how to become a good Christian and a church member. Once you are spiritually born, you don't need to put up with what you received from the first Adam. This has to be deliberate and intentional because it does not happen automatically.

It is not easy to divorce the first Adam with his nature and the consequences of his fall from us. It is like getting a divorce in the natural. I have heard that what people go through in the process of divorce is very painful. It is a hard and painful process to separate yourself from the first Adam and his nature.

The Divine Exchange

Just like we received whatever the first Adam experienced through our natural birth, whatever Christ experienced, we experienced with Him through our spiritual birth. Here are some of the highlights of what Jesus did and experienced on our behalf:

- When Christ obeyed the Father in everything, we obeyed with Him. (Philippians 2:8)
- When Christ fulfilled the Law, we fulfilled it with Him. (Matthew 5:17)
- When Christ was crucified, we were crucified with Him. (Romans 6:6; Galatians 2:20)
- When Christ died, we died with Him. (Romans 6:10; Colossians 2:20, 3:3; 2 Timothy 2:11)
- When Christ was buried, we were buried with Him. (Romans 6:4; Colossians 2:12)
- When Christ was raised from the dead, we were raised with Him. (Ephesians 2:6; Colossians 2:12, 3:1)
- When Christ ascended to heaven, we were ascended with Him. (Ephesians 4:8, 10)
- When Christ was seated at the right hand of God, we were seated in Him. (Ephesians 2:6)
- When Christ defeated the devil, we defeated him with Him. (Colossians 2:15)
- When Christ received all authority in heaven and on earth, we received it with Him. (Matthew 28:18)

Whatever Christ experienced, He did it for us. He became poor for us (2 Corinthians 8:9). He experienced sickness and curses for us. He was rejected and slandered. Now it is our choice to either remain in the first Adam or in the last Adam.

That is why the Bible says, "Therefore, if anyone *is* in Christ, *he is* a new creation; old things have passed away; behold, all things have become new. Now all things *are* of God" (2 Corinthians 5:17–18). The above verse says, "Now all things are of God," not after we die, but now in this present life.

When the Bible says we are a new creation, it means that we have a new DNA. When we are saved, we need to take our lives apart from the DNA level and put them back together according to the original design. This happens through prayer, and by constantly renewing our minds with God's Word by the help of the Holy Spirit and it is a process.

After the resurrection, Jesus made no difference between Himself and the disciples. "Then Jesus said to them, 'Do not be afraid. Go *and* tell My brethren to go to Galilee, and there they will see Me.'" (Matthew 28:10).

Jesus said to her, "Do not cling to Me, for I have not yet ascended to My Father; but go to My brethren and say to them, 'I am ascending to My Father and your Father, and to My God and your God.'" (John 20:17)

For whom He foreknew, He also predestined to *be* conformed to the image of His Son, that He might be the firstborn among many brethren. (Romans 8:29)

When the Bible says "receive Jesus" or "believe in Jesus," it means we are receiving everything He is and all that He has in *exchange* for all the junk and attachments we have with the Babylonian system. But many are not willing to exchange their junk. They keep holding onto it and will even boast about it until they die. Whatever is not of Christ is considered junk, or even dung. The longer we keep it, the more it stinks!

Whatever Christ owns, we own with Him. That is why the Bible says we are co-heirs with Christ. The Father has given all things to Jesus, both in heaven and on earth (John 3:35, 13:3; Romans 8:17; Hebrews 1:2).

I encourage you to pray this prayer to be delivered from the first Adam:

Heavenly Father, I come to You through Jesus Christ, Your Son and my Savior, Lord, and King. Thank You for saving me from everything the fall of the first Adam brought upon my life. Thank You for the blood of Jesus that cleanses me from all my sins. Now, I renounce everything I received from the first Adam through my natural birth. I renounce and sever all damage, defects, and dysfunction that came into my spirit, soul, and DNA through the first Adam. Everything I inherited that was not from You I renounce and cut off from my life and my bloodline in the name of Jesus Christ. Today, I disconnect from my natural bloodline, and I attach myself to the bloodline of Jesus with my whole being. I have a royal bloodline.

I receive everything that is in Christ Jesus. I activate the new life, the new DNA, the new creation, my birthright, and my assignment in Your kingdom, in the name of Jesus Christ. I activate all blessings, qualities, the nature, and the character that is in Christ. I am in Christ. I am a new creation. The old me has passed away. Hallelujah!

We Can Be Born as Sons and Not Fulfill Our Father's Will

As we saw in the parable of the two sons, just because someone is born as a son into the kingdom does not mean that he or she will mature and fulfill their father's assignment. The two individuals in this parable were sons positionally, but they were not matured sons.

God has so many children around the world, but very few sons. Though they are His children, they do not know that He put them on the earth for a reason. Their purpose has been hidden from them. Though they are born into His kingdom, they don't benefit from it because they are not operating in their birthright.

These children can't find provision for their sustenance and resources to fulfill what they want to do. They are living like Gentiles who do not have a Father, but they go to church every Sunday morning.

The Bible talks about other sons of God (angels and spirit beings) who did not keep their proper abode, rebelled against their Father, and were judged and thrown into eternal damnation (Genesis 6:1–7; Job 1:6; Jude 1:6).

The reason the older son worked like a slave was because he had not matured in his sonship. That is why the Bible says that though a person is born as a son, as long as he remains as a child, he is not better than a slave. Though he could have been mature physically, he had not matured in his sonship (Galatians 4:1–5).

The younger son decided to go and do his own thing. Imagine how few people alive today actually fulfill their responsibilities of sonship. That is why the kingdom of God is not manifesting on the earth—and why this world is in such chaos. Most Christians live like they don't belong on the earth because they have not regained their birthright.

This is a prayer to receive your birthright in the kingdom of God:

> Heavenly Father, thank You so much for Your love and mercy through Jesus Christ, Your Son. Thank You for saving me and making me Your son. I receive Jesus as my Lord, Savior, and only King. Thank You so much for restoring my birthright in Your kingdom. I command the enemy to take his hands off of my birthright and all the other rights that came with

it. I receive and activate the Spirit of sonship, my assignment, my authority, and my inheritance as a son in my Father's kingdom. I renounce the orphan heart and all of its syndromes. I command the enemy to restore everything he stole from me and my bloodline since the days of Adam. I am no longer a slave to sin or fear; I am a son of God. Father, thank You for teaching me how to exercise my birthright and for maturing me as a responsible son. In the name of Jesus Christ, I pray. Amen.

Four Stages of Maturity

Not everyone born as a child in the kingdom becomes a matured son or daughter. There are four Greek words used in the Bible for sons based on their levels of maturity. They are similar to the words we use in English—like baby, child, teenager, and adult. The Greek word used in John 1:12 is *teknon*, which is used to indicate offspring, a child, or male child.[3] We are not born as matured sons in the kingdom. We need to grow up and mature, just like we do in the natural. This growth is not physical, but rather emotional and spiritual.

The second Greek word used is found in Galatians 4:1: *nepios*, which refers to an infant, minor, or a little child; someone who is unskilled or who is still in their diapers.[4] Someone needs to take care of these children because they are not able to do anything for themselves.

---

[3] Thayer and Smith, "Greek Lexicon entry for Teknon," The KJV New Testament Greek Lexicon, accessed December 16, 2020, https://www.biblestudytools.com/lexicons/greek/kjv/teknon.html.

[4] Thayer and Smith, "Greek Lexicon entry for Nepios," The KJV New Testament Greek Lexicon, accessed December 16, 2020, https://www.biblestudytools.com/lexicons/greek/kjv/nepios.html.

The third word used is found in John 21:5: *paidion*, which means a young child, a little boy or girl.5 This is what Jesus called His disciples after the resurrection. They went back to fishing and could not catch anything. He appeared to them and called them young children. That was the level of their maturity in understanding His kingdom and His assignment for them at the time.

The fourth Greek word used for an adult *son* is found in Galatians 4:7: *yhios*, which is talking about a man or a matured son.6

We are born into the kingdom as infants. All of us will fit in one of the above stages in our maturity levels toward our sonship in the kingdom. If we are not executing our Father's will on the earth, then we have not matured yet.

Each of these stages requires specific spiritual food for a person to mature and move into the next level, which most people do not receive in a normal church setting. It's similar to what a person requires in the natural. We don't eat baby food when we are an adult. Churches feed every believer with the same food on a Sunday morning; but one person might need the milk of the Word while the next person might require the meat of the Word.

Functioning in Our Sonship

Why does God want us to receive His righteousness to enter His kingdom? Remember, God did not bless Adam for his performance, because he gave tithes, for his singing, or for his spiritual discipline. God blessed him because He is a good Father and He knows what His

---

5 Thayer and Smith, "Greek Lexicon entry for Paidion," The KJV New Testament Greek Lexicon, accessed December 16, 2020, https https://www.biblestudytools.com/lexicons/greek/kjv/paidion.html.

6 James Strong, "G5207 - Yhios," Strong's Greek Lexicon (KJV), Blue Letter Bible, December 16, 2020, https://www.blueletterbible.org/lang/lexicon/lexicon.cfm?ot=KJV&ss=1&strongs=G5207&t=KJV#lexSearch.

sons need before they ask Him. It is the same in the New Testament (Matthew 6:8, 32; 7:11).

Every label and false identity that your race, language, job, nationality, religion, or church affiliation has put on you must be stripped off. How you think about yourself is extremely important; it determines how you will behave to the outside world and if you will be recognized by the spirit world or not. Identity is important in the kingdom; it decides how you behave in your Father's house.

What gave Jesus the courage and confidence to face life, opposition from others, and the devil? It was His identity as a Son of Man and the Son of God. Jesus never called Himself or His disciples "leaders." The name "Son of Man" represents His humanity, and "Son of God" shows His divinity. Each one of us is a son of man and a son of God as well; we need to know when and where to function in those distinct capacities.

The difference between someone having true authority and someone having a title is that the person with authority does not need to impose their position on others or dominate them by the power of their title. Recognition is a natural response to someone who possesses true authority.

May the Lord raise up more kingdom sons on the earth who will execute His will in the nations of the world!

CHAPTER 12

THE PROCESS OF RECEIVING THE FATTED CALF

Though our Father owns the cattle on a thousand hills, many believers around the world are broke and live in survival mode. They are not benefiting from the kingdom because nobody ever taught them how to qualify to receive what they need to fulfill their kingdom assignment.

If you need to receive anything in the kingdom, and for our sonship to work, you need to understand this foundational truth. Everything in the kingdom works around this one revelation that I am about to share with you.

Many go after the fatted calf, meaning material blessings, these days. Most of the messages we hear today are about the fatted calf or how to have more fatted calf. Most believers are not benefiting from the kingdom their Father gave to them. They are functioning as servants, though positionally they are sons.

When we understand the order in which the father gave things to this younger son when he returned home, we receive revelation of the keys to living as a son in God's kingdom and enjoying His blessings. Whatever else we try to do to become sons or to receive from Him and live in His kingdom is a waste of time.

When we come to the door of the kingdom, which is Jesus, everything we have will not come through that door. All of our boasting, degrees, merits, accomplishments, pride, religions, races, and egos will have to stay outside the door if we want to get in. We can circle around the door of the kingdom for forty even eighty years and work hard, thinking we are serving God, but none of those will qualify us. That is why many go after leadership and reject sonship.

In their heads, they think they are sons, but then they boast about their accomplishments, name plates, titles, and degrees. They have not attained the righteousness of God. But if someone did not receive the righteousness of God, then they are not sons, but servants. That is what Jesus said in Matthew:

> But woe to you, scribes and Pharisees, hypocrites! For you shut up the kingdom of heaven against men; for you neither go in *yourselves,* nor do you allow those who are entering to go in. (Matthew 23:13)

It is not easy to live as a son in our Father's kingdom. It is *supposed* to be easy and simple, but we complicate it. When we come to our Father, we have a default mindset that has been programmed by religion, and we slip into it and repeat religious jargon. We think that is what our Father is expecting from us, but that is what we were taught by religion, not the Holy Spirit.

The Holy Spirit is the Spirit of truth; He will always lead us into truth. We need to constantly watch ourselves to keep from slipping into self-righteousness. We will have to fight through it again and again. Our fallen nature love self-righteousness. That is what the devil told us in the beginning. He wanted Adam and Eve to depend on themselves, on their own works to do something apart from God—all to obtain something they already had.

That is what the tree of knowledge of good and evil represented in the garden—self-righteousness. The serpent told them to eat from that tree so that they could "become" something or receive something from God. But they did not need to do anything, they were already like God. He did everything for them.

Remember, Adam did not do anything to become a son or to receive the garden and the entire earth as his inheritance. It was all based on what His Father did for him. He didn't have to do any rituals prior to meeting with God every day. That is why Jesus said in Matthew 5:5, "Blessed *are* the meek, for they shall inherit the earth."

Our Father wants each of us to come to that place in maturity where Adam was, to be able to freely receive His kingdom blessings. If we depend on our accomplishments or self-righteousness, we will forfeit everything God has for us. Many are trying hard to be more holy to receive something that God already prepared and gave to them before the foundation of the earth.

God told Adam that he could *freely* eat of all the trees from the garden. He did not say he had to earn his livelihood by good behavior or hard work. It is the same in the New Testament.

> He who did not spare His own Son, but delivered Him up for us all, how shall He not with Him also freely give us all things? (Romans 8:32)

> Now we have received, not the spirit of the world, but the Spirit who is from God, that we might know the things that have been freely given to us by God. (1 Corinthians 2:12)

To understand the key to receiving the fatted calf, we need to understand the order in which the father gave things to the younger son when he returned home. This order reveals the mystery of sonship and enjoying the fatted calf our Father has for us. When we follow that order in our lives, we won't work for the fatted calf; it will be added to us automatically. As Jesus said, when we seek His kingdom and His righteousness, all the things we need will be added to us.

When the prodigal son came back and the father threw a party for him, he told his servants to bring the best robe to put on him, put a ring on his finger, and sandals on his feet. Then he ordered his servants to kill the fatted calf to prepare the best meal. Each of the things the father gave him represents a position and responsibility we receive in our Father's kingdom as sons. We are going to look in detail at what each one stands for.

Robe of Righteousness

The first thing the father gave when the younger son returned was not the fatted calf, but the best robe he had in his house. This robe could only be worn by special and honorable people or guests. In those days, different functions required different types and colors of robes. By looking at someone's robe, you could tell the position and the authority he carried and the family he belonged to. In the modern day, we have different colored uniforms for different people working in government. We can identify their professions by looking at their uniforms.

The robe represents righteousness. God gives everyone who comes into the kingdom the best robe the robe of righteousness is their first gift.

> I will greatly rejoice in the Lord, my soul shall be joyful in my God; for He has clothed me with the garments of salvation, He has covered me with the robe of righteousness, as a bridegroom decks *himself* with ornaments, and as a bride adorns *herself* with her jewels. (Isaiah 61:10)

We have an option to keep the filthy rags (self-righteousness) that we came in with or to receive the free gift of the robe of righteousness.

THE PROCESS OF RECEIVING THE FATTED CALF

Unfortunately, many do not accept the free gift; they keep their filthy rags. Why? It makes them feel better about themselves, hides their brokenness, or makes them feel like they earned their right standing with God. To accept the free gift, we need to admit our total helplessness, just like the younger son did when he returned.

Many people will not admit their total helplessness because it hurts their pride and egos. They would rather keep bragging about some "torn corner" of their filthy rag that they earned in their own strength many years ago. They keep circumventing the door of the kingdom, but never enter in. They keep saying all the right words and say they want to do the will of God, but they fight against it by their actions—because to do the will of God, they have to surrender their own will and ambitions.

The first thing we need to receive to be a son in God's kingdom is righteousness by faith. Righteousness is what qualifies us to become sons. If we depend on any of our religious works or qualifications of any kind, we will miss His kingdom, sonship, and everything else our Father has in His kingdom for us.

That is why more people are interested in leadership than sonship. Leadership gives them something to boast about, to feel good about themselves. Leadership builds self-reliance, self-confidence, and self-esteem, which produces self-righteousness. Leadership is all about how well I can do something depending on my abilities. Sonship in the kingdom strips away all earthly qualifications and merits we may boast of. The only thing that qualifies us to be children in God's kingdom is His righteousness.

I stumbled over this for many years. I was so self-righteous that I kept missing the mark. God had to rescue me over and over again from my self-righteousness. Thank God for His mercy and grace! I used to claim that I was a born leader. Wherever I went, people appointed me in leadership positions. I felt good about myself, but I was not functioning in my sonship.

The difference between the two sons was in their righteousness. When the younger came back, he put himself at the mercy of his father. He didn't try to say, "Father, I used to be your wonderful son in your home, but I went away for a little while and did some wrong things and I am back now, so please forgive me for what I did, but remember I used to be good." If he had done that, he would not have received anything from his father. His father would have sent him to work with the servants.

The younger son did not have anything to boast about. He said, "I am no longer worthy to be called your son; I have no qualifications whatsoever." We are in the same place spiritually, socially, and racially. We had no qualifications to be sons of God. Only what Jesus did on the cross has qualified us to receive sonship.

In the case of the older son, it was different. He put his trust in his works. He was a great leader.

> So he answered and said to *his* father, "Lo, these many years I have been serving you; I never transgressed your commandment at any time; and yet you never gave me a young goat, that I might make merry with my friends." (Luke 15:29)

This son believed that righteousness came based on what he did. He began to boast about his qualifications—his ability. Unfortunately, the father was not impressed by what he said or did. He did not feel compelled or obligated to give this son anything, because the son did not recognize who his father was and what he expected of him.

The moment we base our worth on natural elements or performance, we disqualify ourselves from being sons in God's kingdom and forfeit everything He has for us. So the first thing the father gave to his younger son was the robe of righteousness. That is what qualifies us to be sons in His kingdom.

What Is the Righteousness of God?

To have the righteousness of God is to come into alignment with God's character, moral standard, holiness, and expectation. It is to be free from the guilt of sin, becoming one with Him by totally depending on what Jesus did for us on the cross, apart from our works and apart from the Law of Moses.

Meeting all the requirements mentioned above is only possible if God does it for us. That is what happened through Jesus Christ. Whatever God expected and required of us, Jesus did in our place so we could receive the free gift of His righteousness, His holiness, and His character by faith.

That is why Jesus told us to seek His kingdom and His righteousness first. As long as we depend on our self-righteousness, we will not enter His kingdom and we will not benefit from it.

The Ring

The second thing this father gave was a ring—the ring of authority to function as a son in his father's house. Again, it was given it to him, but he did not earn it, nor was he qualified to receive it.

The ring represents the authority to conduct business transactions and to enact rules and regulations. In a kingdom, the king uses his signet ring to seal and establish laws and decrees. Once it is sealed by the ring of a king, it becomes the law of the land.

The Sandals

The third thing the father gave to him was the sandals. Only sons wore sandals inside the house of their father. Servants were not allowed to wear sandals inside their master's house. Sandals represent sonship and our birthright.

This is how it was in India. I remember when people came to work in our fields, they did not wear sandals. This was just twenty-five years ago. When people came to work inside the house, they left their sandals or shoes outside the door. Only children had the right to wear shoes inside their father's house.

John 1:12 says, "But as many as received Him, to them He gave the right to become children of God, to those who believe in His name." Based on this verse, what gives us the right to become a child of God? There are two conditions. First, we need to receive Jesus. Many people take this lightly. They think a mere confession will make them a son of God. They put faith in their confession and not in Jesus. They boast about it by saying, "I received Jesus when I was twelve years old, and I have been serving Him for all these years." They have not matured yet.

Saying something like this puts yourself in the category of the older brother in the parable. It is the same thing he told his father. He boasted about how long and well he had been serving his father faithfully and never transgressed his commandments, so he deserved to receive a goat from his father. I will share more about this shortly.

You do not receive Jesus by a mere confession. First of all, we need to know who we were prior to receiving Him. We were lost in sin and never had any qualifications to come before God—we didn't deserve to be treated with mercy. According to the Bible, we were enemies of God (Romans 5:10; Ephesians 2:2–3). The only thing we deserved was His wrath.

When we were enemies, God showed us mercy through Jesus when we only deserved His wrath and punishment. We were condemned to hell; that was our qualification. For anyone to come before God, they need to be righteous. The problem is we did not have any righteousness in us. We could not buy it from the store, nor could we earn it by good works. Somebody had to give it to us. The only righteousness that is approved by God is His righteousness. That is what God did for us through Jesus.

THE PROCESS OF RECEIVING THE FATTED CALF

> But of Him you are in Christ Jesus, who became for us wisdom from God—and righteousness and sanctification and redemption—that, as it is written, "He who glories, let him glory in the Lord." (1 Corinthians 1:30–31)

Jesus became for us the wisdom from God, righteousness, sanctification, and redemption. When the Bible mentions receiving Jesus, it is not just talking about a mere confession. Through that confession, we are admitting something before the court of heaven. We are saying that we are not qualified for this position, but whatever Jesus became for us, we receive that through Him. When we receive Jesus, we are also receiving His righteousness, holiness, position, and authority.

That means when the Father looks at us, Jesus and I have the same righteousness. When the Father looks at us, it is as though Jesus and I have the same status before Him. Thank You, Jesus! This is so powerful, and we need to shout a hallelujah! Many people go after the fatted calf; they want the blessings or the material stuff, but they don't know what qualifies them to receive it.

They begin to use gimmicks and tricks to deceive people to steal from them, promising them all kinds of fatted calf, cars, houses, and wealth. These poor people get scammed by preachers again and again and never receive anything. They go from poor to poorer.

They do that because they do not understand what qualifies them to receive the fatted calf in their father's house. The first thing they need to receive is the gift of righteousness through Jesus and stop depending on their own strength to provide for themselves. All of our boasting has to go. When we depend on our merits, performance, and holiness, we disqualify ourselves from receiving anything from God.

We cannot go after the fatted calf first. We need to go through the divine order that is revealed in this parable, and the fatted calf will be added to us. That is why Jesus instructed us to seek His kingdom and

His righteousness, and then all the things shall be *added to us* not that we would have to work for it. If they are not being added to us, that means we are not following the order revealed above. This is one of the mysteries of the kingdom of God.

According to God, there is none who is righteous not even one who seeks God (see Romans 3:11). That is His report and opinion concerning humanity. But mankind has all kinds of boasting to tell God about how wonderful and good they have been. But none of that can qualify them to enter the kingdom and live as His sons.

What this older son said was a lie. Children cannot boast that they never disobeyed their parents. We have all done a little mischief every now and then. Self-righteousness blinds us from seeing our own weaknesses and failures.

The older son was a very faithful worker. That is what self-righteous people do; they are hard on themselves and committed to the task. They will work more than others, more than the servants, just to prove that they are better and more qualified than the servants.

They have a hard time admitting weakness. While God is saying there is none righteous and not even one who has kept all the commandments, this son says he kept all of them and never transgressed his father. That is a lie; but he cannot see it or admit it because he is blinded by self-righteousness, or the religious spirit.

The Fatted Calf

The fatted calf represents our inheritance, or material blessings. Everything our Father owns belongs to us.

The older son mentioned the goat and fatted calf twice. He was angry at his father for giving the fatted calf to his younger brother, who wasted the father's goods and lived a sinful life. In his perception, he deserved it more than his younger brother. That shows that he did everything so that one day he would receive a goat from his father. However, he did not know what qualified him to receive it.

From the beginning of time, we see people becoming jealous of their brothers' blessings. Cain became angry and jealous at his brother, Abel, because God was pleased with Abel's offering and blessed him. Your blessings cause religious people to become jealous of you.

The phrase *fatted calf* is said three times in this parable. The first time was by the father, the second by the servant, and the third by the older son. Even while the servants were doing their duties, their eyes were on the master's fatted calf. They hoped that one day they would have worked hard enough to be able to afford one.

What this servant and the older son did not understand is what qualified the younger son to receive it. He received it for free—not based on his works. He never asked his father for a fatted calf. Neither the servant nor the older son said anything about the other three things the father gave to the younger son; they were hidden from them. They did not understand the meaning of the things this father gave his younger son. That is the mystery of receiving what we need in the kingdom of God.

Even today, many people's eyes are on the fatted calf. They are working, praying, serving, preaching, pastoring, sowing, singing, and shouting and their goal is to have the fatted calf. The sad thing is that it was theirs from the very beginning; they inherited it by their birth into their father's house or kingdom. But they never realized it because they had the wrong perception of their father and about their birthright.

Why are our identities as sons important in the kingdom? That is what we are going to look at in the next chapter.

CHAPTER 13
MANIFESTATION OF THE SONS OF GOD

From the beginning of time, God only wanted sons—not Jews and Gentiles, not leaders, not Pentecostals and Baptists and Catholics. We have plenty of those, but very few sons. God restored the status of sonship to the Gentiles through Jesus Christ. He came to reveal the heart of God to the world.

Any label or identity you have except as a son of God in His kingdom is demonically influenced and is a substitute. The only relationship God ever wanted between Him and humans is a Father-and-son relationship in His kingdom. This was His original design from the beginning and not an identity based on race, nationality, language, title, position, education, profession, religion, caste, ritual, or denomination. They all must go when we accept sonship in our Father's kingdom.

People go after titles and positions because they are not secure in their sonship in the kingdom.

Sonship

What helps us mature as sons in the kingdom? What gives us confidence toward God to execute His will on His behalf? It is the knowledge and the understanding of His purpose and character that matures a person in the kingdom. The more we know God's purpose, patterns (ways), plans, principles, and character, the more we will know Him. The more we know Him, the more mature and confident we become toward Him and about our identity as children in the kingdom.

When Father God wrote the final will and gave everything to His Son, Jesus, do you know what He did? He included our names in that will. That is why the Bible says we are co-heirs with Christ. This means everything Christ owns, we own them with Him. We are seated in Him, not below Him or above Him or beside Him, but *in* Him (see Ephesians 2:6). We have been made one spirit with Him (1 Corinthians 6:17). We reign with Him, not under Him or for Him.

Do you want to know everything Christ owns?

> Jesus, knowing that the Father had given all things into His hands, and that He had come from God and was going to God. (John 13:3)

> [God] has in these last days spoken to us by *His* Son, whom He has appointed heir of all things, through whom also He made the worlds. (Hebrews 1:2)

We are joint heirs with Christ.

> The Spirit Himself bears witness with our spirit that we are children of God, and if children, then heirs—heirs of God and joint heirs with Christ, if indeed we suffer with *Him*, that we may also be glorified together. (Romans 8:16–17)

That is why the devil hates the revelation of sonship. He doesn't want the heirs rising up and stripping him of his illegal possession of our inheritance or his illicit operation. He has been running an illegal kingdom for too long. He is not authorized to do what he is doing. He can continue only as long as he keeps mankind blinded from their sonship in their Father's kingdom.

> For the earnest expectation of the creation eagerly waits for the revealing of the sons of God. (Romans 8:19)

Why is all creation waiting for the manifestation of the sons of God? It is because creation only recognizes sons, not servants or Pentecostals. This earth and everything in it were given to the sons of God as an inheritance from their Father. The devil hates the sons of God. He doesn't want anyone to come into the revelation of sonship. As long as people put themselves under different religious and social labels, the devil will not care or lose much.

The moment you begin to function as a son in the kingdom and begin to reclaim what is legally yours, then you will see his reaction. The demonic world only recognizes the sons of God and not Pentecostals or charismatics, and not the sons of some preachers or bishops. That is why when Jesus was declared as a Son at His baptism by His Father, He had to go through a series of tests to prove that He really believed it.

Soon after Jesus was declared a beloved Son by the Father, the devil came to Him with temptations, and the first thing the enemy questioned was His identity. There is no record of Satan coming to Jesus before He was declared a Son.

Satan said, "*If* you are the Son of God." He did not say, "If You are a great leader," "If You are an apostle or a prophet," or even, "If You are a holy Jew." Note that the question was about His sonship. That is why the enemy fights as hard as he can to hide or distort your identity in the kingdom. The devil does not care how many leaders are on this planet; he is looking for sons. He hates them because they are a threat to his operation. Sons are the legal heirs of God's property. The devil is the illegal heir. God did not give this planet to the devil; we gave it to him. Actually, he stole it from us through deception.

The reason all creation is waiting for the manifestation of the sons of God is because we are the legal heirs of everything God created. God entrusted us with the earth and everything in it. The creation has been under the bondage of corruption for so long. God set us free, but we haven't come to the full revelation of what it really means to function as a son of God on the earth. Creation has been groaning until now because we have a responsibility toward it. God entrusted it to us, and we gave it to the devil, subjecting it to bondage and bringing it under corruption.

> For the earnest expectation of the creation eagerly waits for the revealing of the sons of God. For the creation was subjected to futility, not willingly, but because of Him who subjected *it* in hope; because the creation itself also will be delivered from the bondage of corruption into the glorious liberty of the children of God. For we know that the whole creation groans and labors with birth pangs together until now. (Romans 8:19–22)

Creation is not waiting for revival fire or fire from heaven to burn, as we were taught. It is waiting and groaning for freedom. It is experiencing birth pangs, groaning to become everything God created it to be. But creation was brought under corruption because of our failure and fall. What it is waiting for is the glorious liberty of the children of God—waiting for us to receive the revelation of sonship and fulfill our responsibilities in our Father's kingdom.

> You have made him to have dominion over the works of Your hands; you have put all things under his feet. (Psalm 8:6)

The verse above is talking about mankind. God has made us to have dominion over the works of His hands and put all things under our feet. The reason we are not seeing everything under our feet is because we are not functioning as sons of God on earth. We have been divided into different factions based on our color, dress code, and particular belief systems and doctrines. This will only change when mankind recognizes their kingdom identity of sonship.

SEVEN REASONS WHY SONSHIP IS IMPORTANT IN THE KINGDOM

1. The Father Is Looking for Sons

This is the kind of relationship God wanted to have with us from the beginning of time. Adam was His son (Luke 3:38). The devil hates sons because they are the heirs. As long as he can keep believers blinded from their sonship, he wins and can keep our inheritance and use people for building his kingdom.

> I will be a Father to you, and you shall be My sons and daughters, says the Lord Almighty. (2 Corinthians 6:18)

The Father is not looking for more Christians, leaders, believers, or even fivefold ministry gifts. Everything in the kingdom flows from the foundation of our relationship with Him as sons. Apostles, prophets, and all other ministry gifts are functions in the church. You do not relate with God as an apostle or a pastor, but as a son.

2. Creation Only Recognizes Sons

The moment you receive the spirit of sonship, your view of creation and your relationship with it changes, as well as how creation relates to you. You will begin to appreciate the works and creation of God your Father. Most Christians do not care about creation; they are waiting for everything to be burned and for them to fly away. Because they themselves are not free from the spirit of bondage that brings fear (Romans 8:15), they have no care for creation. But creation is waiting for the manifestation of the sons of God (Romans 8:19).

That is why the Bible says, "Therefore if the Son makes you free, you shall be free indeed' (John 8:36). Only sons have the authority to set people and creation free. It is interesting to notice that this verse did not say, "Whom Jesus set free," but "Whom the Son set free."

One of the scariest verses in the New Testament is Revelation 11:18, where it declares that when Jesus comes, He will destroy those who destroy the earth. If we do not take good care of the property God entrusted us with, we will face severe punishment when He comes.

3. The Demonic World Only Recognizes the Authority of Sons

The devil does not care whether you are an apostle, a doctor, worship leader, or even a pastor. What he cares about is if you are walking in the authority of your sonship. When Jesus cast out demons, they came out of people saying, "You are the Christ, the Son of God!" (Luke 4:41). They didn't say He was the great apostle, a prophet, or the most holy Jew on the planet. They only recognized His sonship.

Evil spirits testified of Paul as a son, not an apostle, saying, "Paul I know" (Acts 19:15). They did not say they know who the Apostle Paul is. Apostleship is a function, and sonship is our position. Position determines our authority.

4. The Father Only Approves and Releases Sons

Many are waiting to be released to fulfill their destiny in the kingdom, but they do not understand what is holding them back. They think that God does not love them enough or that they made some mistakes. The reality is that they have not matured into sons yet. He is waiting for us, not the other way around!

They have waited for decades and have not been released to fulfill their assignment. They thought they needed more training in leadership, had to become more spiritual, required a seminary degree, or had to obtain some other special skills or gifts. Some believe they need to be connected with some famous preacher. No. What they need is the revelation of their sonship in the kingdom.

The Father only releases sons to do business for Him and on behalf of Him, and to represent Him.

The Father sends the Son or the sons. Those sons who are *sent* are called apostles. Jesus had to wait thirty years for His Father to release Him to fulfill His destiny. When He turned thirty years old, He was ready to fulfill His function as a Son. Throughout the Gospels, we read that Jesus only addressed Himself as a Son.

The Bible says that the Father sent His Son to the world. Jesus was born as a baby and He had to grow up. The Bible also says Jesus grew in wisdom and in stature, and in favor with God and men (Luke 2:52). It took time for Him to grow and mature.

The Father put the seal on His Son and upon His sons.

> Do not labor for the food which perishes, but for the food which endures to everlasting life, which the Son of Man will give you, because God the Father has set His seal on Him. (John 6:27)

God the Father has put His seal on His sons. The Greek word used for *seal* is *sphragizo*, which means "to set a seal upon *for security, to hide, to set apart, in order to prove.*"[7] This seal is for protection from Satan

---

[7] Thayer and Smith, "Greek Lexicon entry for Sphragizo," The KJV New Testament Greek Lexicon, accessed November 15, 2020, https://www.biblestudytools.com/lexicons/greek/kjv/sphragizo.html.

and to hide from people who shouldn't be seeing you or knowing who you are. It means to be set apart for a particular use or a special day, and lastly, to prove to others your worth and who you are in the Spirit. This is powerful to understand!

While Jesus was waiting those thirty years to be released to fulfill His kingdom assignment, He was being prepared to function as the Son. Remember, He was human like we are, but without sin. It was not easy for Jesus to empty Himself and totally submit to His Father. It took Him thirty years to reach that point.

The Bible says that He learned obedience through the things He suffered. We are in that process as well. The more we prepare to obey the Father and are ready to do His will, the more we will function in our sonship in the kingdom.

> Who, in the days of His flesh, when He had offered up prayers and supplications, with vehement cries and tears to Him who was able to save Him from death, and was heard because of His godly fear, though He was a Son, *yet* He learned obedience by the things which He suffered. (Hebrews 5:7–8)

We have to remember that it wasn't easy for Jesus to learn obedience to His Father just because He was the Son of God. He struggled with it! Remember the battle He had to face in the garden of Gethsemane? He was sweating blood because of the intense pressure He was under.

5. The Kingdom Belongs to the Sons

The kingdom belongs to sons, and that is why the Bible call us "sons of the kingdom" (see Matthew 8:12; 13:38). As I mentioned earlier, everything God created has a purpose, a place, and a function built in to fulfill that purpose. God's sons are supposed to be in His kingdom; it is their birthright and their inheritance. The kingdom is an inheritance to the sons from their Father (Matthew 25:34).

6. Inheritance Belongs to the Sons

In a family or kingdom, only sons receive the father's inheritance. Servants and slaves receive gifts. Sons get to inherit their father's kingdom, throne, and wealth. It is possible to serve God and be struggling to survive if you are acting like a slave. But a son will not struggle to survive in his Father's house. Remember the parable of the prodigal son and his brother? Though they were sons, they were struggling because they did not recognize who they were and who their father was.

7. Sonship Is the Solution to Overcome Fear

Once you begin to relate with God as your Abba Father, your fear of the devil, fear of losing salvation, fear of people, and fear of the unknown or tomorrow vanishes. As long as we operate in the spirit of fear or the spirit of bondage, as it says in Romans 8:15, we will have no confidence toward God. Sonship should give you confidence, not your leadership skills. God sent Jesus so we can serve Him without fear all the days of our life (Luke 1:74–75).

That is why Jesus said our heavenly Father knows what we have need of before we ask Him (Matthew 6:8, 32). If we understand that our Father knows what we need, it helps us to stop worrying.

The first thing we should teach new believers when they get saved is about the kingdom and their sonship in the kingdom, not about leadership. The first thing we should see when we are born again is the kingdom of God. The first "right" or privilege we receive from the Father is the right to be His children (John 1:12).

Only once a person is grounded and established on the revelation of their sonship should we teach them about church, calling, ministry, gifts of the Holy Spirit, the fivefold ministry gifts, and everything else.

Otherwise, they will go out and build their own kingdoms instead of God's kingdom, because their identities have not been settled yet. Most of the gimmicks people do in ministry are because of their insecurities, hunger for position, and for the love of money. They are not aware of their true identities and do not know their inheritance as God's children.

The Third Son

There was a third son in this parable—the Son who is sharing it. He is the perfect Son of God who came to do the will of His Father, even to the extent of giving His own life by going to the cross. He came to reveal the true heart of the Father toward humans. He came with the message of the kingdom, which is the will of His Father from the beginning. We need to follow the footsteps of that Son, not the Gentiles or Jewish roots.

When the first son, Adam, failed, God sent another Adam, called the Last Adam, to show us how to live as sons in our Father's kingdom. Just like whatever happened to the first Adam happened to the rest of humanity, whatever happened to the Last Adam (Jesus) happened to the rest of humanity who believes it. This is the gist of the entire Bible.

How did Jesus address Himself? Did He ever mention His natural heritage? Which tribe or race did He belong to? He always called Himself the "Son of Man" or the "Son of God." When we come into the kingdom, that should be our identity as well.

If you are a son of God, you will receive and understand the message of the kingdom. If people are ruled by the religious spirit and self-righteousness, they will reject sonship and the message of the kingdom; it won't make any sense to them. It did not make any sense to the Jewish religious leaders, either. Performing another religious ritual, completing a religious duty, or singing another song for their Father was their mantra.

They will keep quoting verses from the Bible like the Pharisees did to Jesus, trying to prove they were right and Jesus was wrong with His kingdom teaching. This keeps happening. Lord, have mercy!

Jesus shared another parable of two sons:

> But what do you think? A man had two sons, and he came to the first and said, "Son, go, work today in my vineyard." He answered and said, "I will not," but afterward he regretted it and went. Then he came to the second and said likewise. And he answered and said, "I *go*, sir," but he did not go. Which of the two did the will of *his* father?
>
> They said to Him, "The first."
>
> Jesus said to them, "Assuredly, I say to you that tax collectors and harlots enter the kingdom of God before you. For John came to you in the way of righteousness, and you did not believe him; but tax collectors and harlots believed him; and when you saw *it*, you did not afterward relent and believe him." (Matthew 21:28–32)

Jesus is talking again about two sons, and they represent the sinners and the religious leaders. The sinners did not feel worthy to be used by God; at first, they resisted, but later they obeyed. They are the first son who said he would not go to his father's vineyard, but later repented and went. The second son represents the religious group; they said they would do anything and would obey all God's commandments, but then later they rebelled and disobeyed. The vineyard here represents the earth, not ministry or the church.

Jesus asked them which one did the will of their father. They said it was the first. He was showing what was going to happen—that the tax collectors and harlots would enter the kingdom of God before the religious leaders. From the beginning, God has been concerned only about His will and plan, which is to see His kingdom established on this earth.

The Real Reason Why the Devil Killed Jesus

Do you want to know the real reason why the devil killed Jesus through the Jewish leaders? It was not because He healed people, prophesied the destruction of their temple, or even for preaching the gospel of the kingdom. They killed Him for one reason because of His claim to Sonship. He is the heir.

In Luke 22:66–71, we read that the Jewish religious leaders questioned Jesus about His identity. They asked Him if He was the Christ. He said, "Hereafter the Son of Man will sit on the right hand of the power of God." For that they asked if He was the Son of God. He replied and said, "You rightly say that I am." When they heard that, they became angry, and the high priest even tore his clothes (Matthew 26:65).

It was the Sonship of Jesus in His Father's kingdom that threatened the devil and his demons. The demonic kingdom hates any son of God who claims their position on earth. They killed Jesus because He is the legal heir of this earth and the throne of David, who would rule this earth.

Jesus shared a parable about this:

> "Hear another parable: There was a certain landowner who planted a vineyard and set a hedge around it, dug a winepress in it and built a tower. And he leased it to vinedressers and went into a far country. Now when vintage-time drew near, he sent his servants to the vinedressers, that they might receive its

> fruit. And the vinedressers took his servants, beat one, killed one, and stoned another. Again he sent other servants, more than the first, and they did likewise to them. Then last of all he sent his son to them, saying, 'They will respect my son.' But when the vinedressers saw the son, they said among themselves, 'This is the heir. Come, let us kill him and seize his inheritance.' So they took him and cast *him* out of the vineyard and killed *him*.
>
> "Therefore, when the owner of the vineyard comes, what will he do to those vinedressers?"
>
> They said to Him, "He will destroy those wicked men miserably, and lease *his* vineyard to other vinedressers who will render to him the fruits in their seasons." (Matthew 21:33–41)

When Jesus revealed His true identity, the religious leaders could not accept it. The religious system will always fight against sonship, and they won't teach you about it, either. They want to keep people enslaved to their rituals and systems, and they will use you to benefit themselves. The religious leaders in Jesus' day became angry with Him and gave Him up to be crucified.

Why the Devil Hates Sonship So Much

There are many reasons why the devil hates sonship. When we discover our sonship, he gets scared. Imagine what it would be like if all Christians began to walk in the revelation and authority of their sonship; there would be nothing we could not accomplish for the kingdom!

Here are a few of the reasons why the devil hates sonship so much:

- Sons are the heirs of their father's inheritance
- Sons are the heirs of their father's possessions
- Only sons have the authority to question any intruders or trespassers
- Only sons have the right to conduct business transactions on behalf of their father
- Sons carry the image and likeness of their father
- Sons are representatives of their father
- The earth was given to the sons of God (Luke 3:38)

These are the same reasons the religious leaders killed Stephen. When Stephen said he saw the heaven opened and the Son of Man standing at the right hand of God, the religious mob became angry and they stoned him to death (Acts 7:55–60).

The revelation of sonship is one of the most crucial keys for unlocking the potential of the kingdom of God and its provision in people's lives. Once people learn that they are sons who are inheriting the kingdom, and not just slaves working for God for the rest of their lives, it will free them to become who God has called them to be. This is why I teach so much about sonship and its importance in the kingdom.

CHAPTER 14

LEADERSHIP VS. SONSHIP

The Bible is not a book about leadership; it is a book about sonship and the sons' assignment in their Father's kingdom. God did not write the Bible to teach us leadership principles, but to reveal His purpose for our lives and why He created the earth and put mankind on it.

There is great emphasis on leadership among Christians and church people today. Even some kingdom people fall prey to it because it looks so attractive to their flesh. But Jesus did not come to turn followers into leaders; that was not His life mission, nor was it the purpose of His coming. His mission was to turn slaves into sons. His sons had been taken captive by an enemy kingdom, and He came to restore them. His kingdom is not about leadership, but about sonship.

Many think Jesus was the greatest leader who ever lived. They have written books about it and made millions of dollars from them. They started training programs and leadership schools, but Jesus did not come to teach us about leadership. He was not a leader; He was a Son who came to do the will of His Father. The only time the word leader is used in the New Testament is to talk about the Jewish religious leaders.

Jesus never stamped Himself with any title. To my knowledge, when He was talking about Himself, He didn't even use His own name. Every time He addressed Himself, He said, "Son of Man," "The Son," or "Son of God." That was His title. He wanted to show the world what sonship is all about. God created us to be His sons, and Adam was His first son on earth (Luke 3:38). But when Adam lost his sonship because of disobedience, God had to send another Son to show us how sons live in their Father's kingdom.

We have plenty of great leaders around us, but we have very few sons. All creation is waiting, not for the manifestation of great leaders, but for the manifestation of the sons of God. There is a huge difference between leadership and sonship.

Comparing Leadership and Sonship

When mankind lost the kingdom of God, the devil gave us the Babylonian system. When we lost our relationship with the Father, the devil gave us religion and rituals. When we lost sonship, the devil gave us a counterfeit concept called "leadership." When we lost our kingdom assignments, the enemy brought survival mentality and employment. When we lost the joy of being with our Father and doing His will, the enemy gave us fun and entertainment to keep us busy.

Leadership is a Babylonian concept, while sonship is a kingdom concept. The idea of leadership came from the search for significance. People like to feel significant, and they will do anything to feel that. Nobody taught us about birthright and how to live and function as sons in our Father's kingdom and fulfill our kingdom assignment.

Leadership is ambitious and is always looking for how to become successful. Sonship is not about success; it is about doing your Father's will, doing what you have been sent here to do. That is what Jesus came to show. Every son in the kingdom starts as a leader. But he or she should not stop there; they have to grow into maturity of a son in the kingdom.

Below are some of the comparisons between leadership and sonship.

Leadership Focuses On:	Sonship Focuses On:
Position	Serving
What you can achieve	What you can inherit or receive
Knowledge and being right	Humility and meekness
Achieving dreams and goals	Fulfilling your Father's assignment
Learning first	Unlearning first
Influence	Obedience
Attitude	Aptitude
Solving problems	Fulfilling purpose and establishing the Father's kingdom
How successful you become at the end	How much of God's will was established because you arrived on this planet
Outward looks	Who you are inside
Who you know	How much you know about sonship
Who knows you	Who you are
Your personality type	Your character
Positioning yourself	God's timing
Information	Maturity
Communication skills	Listening
Leaving your own legacy	Your Father's kingdom

Leadership Focuses On:	Sonship Focuses On:
Self-importance	Dying to self to do the Father's will
Power	Purpose
Who is in the front	Where each one fits
Productivity	Stewardship
Accomplishing a task or getting things done	Functioning in the original design
Leading	Showing how things are supposed to be done and empowering
Who gets the credit	God gets all the credit
Self-exaltation	Exalting the Father
Who gets there first	Everyone fulfilling their specific calling
Can be a hired position	An heir; an inherited position, never hired
Possessing great qualities	Manifesting the image and likeness of the Father
Where we are going	Where we came from
Transaction	Function
Teamwork	Family
Tasks	Relationship
From Babylon	From the kingdom of God
Becoming someone great and famous	Becoming like the Father

Leadership Focuses On:	Sonship Focuses On:
Finding and having more followers	Raising up more sons
Gaining confidence	The kingdom solution for overcoming fear
Significance	Purpose
Self	The Father and His will

The first man God ever created was a son. The leadership theory came from the Babylonian system to corrupt the minds of the sons with worldly ambition for power, position, wealth, influence, and success. Just like the Romans took the ekklesia and turned it into a religious system called the church, the Babylonian system took sonship and turned it into leadership.

Meanwhile, the Spirit of sonship is from Jesus Christ and His kingdom. The Father is looking for sons on earth not for more leaders. Leaders are looking to be successful, but sonship is not about being successful. Sons are here to do their Father's will. It is about seeing what the Father is doing and copying it on earth as it is in heaven.

When people lost their kingdom assignment in the fall, they came up with ways to feel significant. As a result of the search for significance, people began to focus more on leadership and less on sonship. When Adam fell, he lost sonship, and the devil came up with the idea of leadership as a substitute.

If you look at the body of Christ today, there is so much talk and training on leadership, but very little training and teaching on sonship. The devil is not worried about how many leaders are out there, because most of them are already slaves to his system. He is only afraid of sons. That is why the demonic world recognized Jesus as the Son of God, not as a great leader. They came out of people not because of His leadership qualities, but because of the authority He carried in the Spirit as the Son of Man.

> For it was fitting for Him, for whom are all things and by whom are all things, in bringing many sons to glory, to make the captain of their salvation perfect through sufferings. (Hebrews 2:10)

The verse above says Jesus brought many sons to glory, not to great leadership. We have so many great leaders today that the demonic world does not recognize because they are not walking in the authority of their sonship in the kingdom. They have the spirit of leadership, but not the Spirit of sonship. I will say it again: this world doesn't need more leaders, but more sons of God!

Jesus Had to Extract the Spirit of Leadership

The disciples had this spirit in the beginning of their training in the kingdom to become sons. They came to Jesus asking for positions, rewards, and revenge; they wanted to bring fire down from heaven and destroy the lives of others. That is the spirit of Babylon.

In the beginning, until they discovered their sonship and began to function in it, there was an argument among the disciples about who was the greatest among them. Jesus' response was to tell them that their spirit was not of Him and that theirs was the kind of spirit they saw among the Gentiles who lorded it over people and wanted to rule over them.

Jesus replied and said, "It shall not be so among you." There should not be any leadership position in the kingdom. The kingdom operates by sons who know their functions and their specific places in the kingdom.

> And when His disciples James and John saw this, they said, "Lord, do You want us to command fire to come down from heaven and consume them, just as Elijah did?" But He turned and rebuked them, and said, "You do not know what manner of spirit you are of." (Luke 9:54–55)

> But Jesus called them to Himself and said, "You know that the rulers of the Gentiles lord it over them, and those who are great exercise authority over them. Yet it shall not be so among you; but whoever desires to become great among you, let him be your servant." (Matthew 20:25–26)

Leadership looks so attractive to the natural man. Who wouldn't like to be successful and influential on the earth? If you are a leader, I would encourage you to renounce the spirit of leadership and receive the Spirit of sonship into your heart (Romans 8:15; Galatians 4:1-7).

The kingdom way of meeting the need to feel significant is by fulfilling your purpose and flowing in your calling. When you do that, you will automatically feel significant, and others will need you and will come looking for you. Walking in your specific calling is the kingdom way of feeling significant and meeting all our needs.

Leadership is a deception of the enemy that is designed to keep believers from entering their sonship in the kingdom. As long as the enemy can keep the sons of the kingdom from operating in their authority and receiving the inheritance their Father has for them, he has won his battle over them.

The enemy does not care what type of leader you are and what leadership style you express as an individual. As long as he can keep your birthright, your inheritance in the kingdom, and keep you a slave to the Babylonian system by serving money and chasing fame and success—he is happy.

One interesting thing I found is not everyone who is born into the kingdom becomes a son. That might shock you. The opportunity is given to everyone, but not everyone reaches that maturity. The Bible says in John 1:12 that God has given authority to anyone who believes and receives Jesus to become a child of God, just like the two sons we saw in the parable.

Some translations say, "sons of God." The Greek word used there is teknon, which means a little child, not a matured son.[8] Everyone who is born of God is a child of God, but very few mature to become sons. It takes maturity and responsibility to become a son and carry out the task the Father wants us to accomplish.

When Jesus talks about Himself, He refers to Himself as a Son, not a leader. I could not find a single reference where He says His own name. He always says, "Son of Man" or just "Son."

Then Jesus answered and said to them, "Most assuredly, I say to you, the Son can do nothing of Himself, but what He sees the Father do; for whatever He does, the Son also does in like manner." (John 5:19)

That is what we should be referring to ourselves; as sons of God. Instead, we have come up with all kinds of titles and positions.

Why the Spirit of Sonship?

> And because you are sons, God has sent forth the Spirit of His Son into your hearts, crying out, "Abba, Father!" (Galatians 4:6)

> For you did not receive the spirit of bondage again to fear, but you received the Spirit of adoption by whom we cry out, "Abba, Father." The Spirit Himself

---

[8] Thayer and Smith, "Greek Lexicon entry for Teknon," The KJV New Testament Greek Lexicon, accessed December 16, 2020, https://www.biblestudytools.com/lexicons/greek/kjv/teknon.html.

bears witness with our spirit that we are children of God. (Romans 8:15–16)

The Bible talks about the Spirit of sonship, and not daughtership. When God took Eve out of Adam, the same spirit that was in Adam went into Eve. She did not receive a lesser spirit in any way or form. She did not receive a male spirit, but a human spirit. There is no male or female spirit, but human spirit. There are male or female bodies or genders. Adam was the son of God, so the same spirit of sonship he had went into Eve.

When we are born again, we receive the Spirit of sonship from Jesus. We are the bride of Christ, like Eve was to Adam. The same Spirit that is in Jesus came into us. That is why the Bible says, "Now if anyone does not have the Spirit of Christ, he is not His" (Romans 8:9b).

Though Eve was taken out of Adam, they were different in many ways. Men and women are different physically, emotionally, sexually, and in our natures. God created us to do different things and to fulfill different roles in life. We were not created to do the same things in life. Man was created to do things a woman cannot do, and in the same way, the woman was created to do the things a man cannot do. We should appreciate and celebrate the differences!

The Importance of Sonship

The devil is not worried about how many leaders are out there or how many leaders we train or raise up. What we need to do is to train believers how to regain their sonship and functions in their kingdom identity. Only sons can execute the Father's will. The kingdom is available only for the sons of God (Matthew 13:38). Only sons are a threat to the devil and his kingdom—only sons receive their Father's inheritance.

Neither God nor the devil are worried about or interested to know how many Christians are in a country or how many members a church has. What God wants to know is how many of them are living in sonship. He is looking for sons, not more converts. What the devil is afraid of is the sons of God. Only they are a threat to him and his kingdom.

Only a son can understand the heart and the mission of a father. A servant or a slave is a liability to the master, even though they accomplish some tasks for him. Leaders are neither a liability nor a blessing to the Father. They are out there following their own ambitions and dreams and trying to become someone great. A son is an asset and an heir. Whatever the father invests in a son will be of future benefit to the family.

Once we recognize our birthright and identity as sons in the kingdom of our Father, the devil's business is finished. That is why the devil keeps encouraging and promoting Christians worldwide to go after leadership and other nonsense. As long as he can keep them busy and distracted pursuing leadership positions, he will do it.

That is why the Bible says Jesus led many sons into glory (Hebrews 2:10). We will go after leadership and deaconship until we discover our identity as sons in the kingdom. Many go after leadership and pay huge amounts of money to be trained as a leader under someone because of the identity crisis. People want to feel important and significant. They think leadership will make them feel significant and important in front of others or it will position them in this world.

The secret to feeling significant and to receiving what we need is to fulfill the responsibility of our sonship in the kingdom. When you discover yourself as a son and fulfill what you are called to do in the kingdom, you will automatically feel significant and will not lack anything in your life. When you operate in the gifts God gave you, it will make room for you in this world (Proverbs 18:16).

When Jesus was baptized, the Father did not make an announcement from heaven saying, "Ladies and gentlemen, I am so proud to present you the greatest leader this world has ever seen, Jesus Christ of Nazareth!" Instead, He said, "This is My beloved Son, in whom I am well pleased" (Matthew 3:17). That is the same identity we have in His kingdom. Every other identity is false.

What this world needs is not more leaders, but sons—sons of God who can manifest the image and likeness of their Father to the rest of the world and creation; sons of God who can manifest the kingdom of God to the natural world. The Bible says in John 1:12 that God has given the authority to anyone who believes in Jesus to become a child of God and not a Pentecostal, Baptist, or a Catholic. Those are the labels the religious spirit puts on people.

Once we are settled in our identity as sons and daughters of God, we move into the next step of living in the original design God has for us. If we move into the next step before our identity is settled, many will get offended at God during the process and try to run away. The next chapter is about the stages we will have to through in order to live in God's original design.

CHAPTER 15

TEN STAGES OF DISCIPLESHIP

Since Jesus gave us the kingdom two thousand years ago, why haven't we discipled at least one whole nation, or even a town, yet? The early disciples reached the entire known world with the gospel of the kingdom in their lifetime and discipled many countries in the Middle East.

The reason we have not been able to do this is because we have not had the full gospel. We thought we had the full gospel, but it wasn't full at all—only a fragment. Each person and each group went forward with what they knew and had, but many were doing it for their own bellies or for a position.

Other religious groups have discipled nations and cities, while we have been waiting for a rapture and another revival so we can *feel* God. All the while, the enemy stole our nations from us.

These other religious groups were not waiting for a revival. They took over our educational systems, media, governments, and economies without any revival. They had a plan and a strategy. If we do not learn from God, we should at least look at the enemy and see how a kingdom operates. The devil copies God in everything because he knows how He operates better than most preachers or seminary professors do.

The purpose of kingdom discipleship is to release a person to fulfill his or her kingdom assignment. That is what Jesus did for these fishermen. He did not lay hands on them and then they became the greatest apostles in a day. He trained them for more than three years. He trained them to know how to fulfill their assignment. Every other form of discipleship is geared toward making a person more religious.

Before Jesus can release us to disciple nations, we have to go through the same process He took His early disciples through. Only when we complete all of these stages can God release us to go and disciple nations like Jesus did with His disciples.

This is an important segment of this book and the entire kingdom school courses. If we miss this, nothing else will work for us in the kingdom. May the Holy Spirit minister to your hearts as you read the following pages.

We Need to Shift from Selfish Ambitions to Kingdom Building

There are four ways to live our lives or to serve God. The first one is under the influence of the religious spirit. The second way to live is for our survival. The third way to live is to fulfill our selfish ambitions. The fourth way to live or serve God is by doing our kingdom assignment.

Many people have twisted the kingdom teaching and made it all about becoming successful and making money. It is not easy to live a kingdom life. You need to die to yourself and all of your personal and selfish ambitions. You are signing up to be martyred for the King if need be.

People have brought worldly concepts of success and leadership into the kingdom. Kingdom life is only for *dead* people—those who are dead to their flesh and ambitions. Like Paul said, "I have been crucified with Christ; it is no longer I who live, but Christ lives in me." (Galatians 2:20)

Some people take the promises Jesus made to His disciples about if anyone leaves land, houses, father, mother, etc., they will receive it back a hundredfold. But that is only part of the story. What about dying for Him or taking up His cross and following Him daily (Luke 9:23)?

When we come into the kingdom, we will no longer live to achieve our dreams and ambitions. From that moment on, we accept His will and His dream as ours, and follow Him daily. We accept His kingdom assignment to be carried out through our lives.

We need to be careful to not let the Babylonian concept of success and fame creep into our hearts. Remember the first king of Babylon? His name was Nimrod, and he became famous and successful through his hunting ability. He was the first human hero on the earth, and people began to worship him. That spirit is still prevalent today. Unfortunately, it crept into the body of Christ as well. People are more excited about their sports teams and superstars than they are about Jesus and His kingdom.

You do not come into the kingdom to become a leader. You come into the kingdom to become a son and to fulfill your kingdom assignment, whatever that might be. It might be cleaning the toilet and if you are called to do that, you need to do it unto the Lord, not to please a leader.

You may ask, "Isn't the kingdom of God all about building and discipling nations?" Yes, it is, but we need to be careful how we build it. We have a long way to go to prepare for it. The church has not raised up people to take their positions in different spheres of life; instead, we taught them how to sing and how to do church.

We have not raised up any judges, Supreme Court justices, presidents, mayors, or governors. We need to raise up educators and professors. We need to raise up some kingdom citizens who are free from greed and covetousness and who are free from the hunger for power, position, and money.

Before Jesus released the disciples to go and disciple nations, He had to take them through a process of training. That is what we do through our Kingdom School. Jesus enrolled these twelve men into His kingdom school and walked with them stage by stage.

THE TEN-STAGE PROCESS TO PREPARE FOR THE KINGDOM ASSIGNMENT

When we study in detail, we see that the disciples had to go through ten stages before they finished their training. I am going to cover each of those stages in a nutshell. Each of us needs to go through this process in order to be ready to fulfill our kingdom assignment. Each stage had to do with a specific selfish or personal ambition they had in their hearts.

The disciples had to go through a process before they became the apostles Jesus wanted them to be. The first ambition they had to die to was the desire to become rich. As fishermen, they dreamed about catching the biggest catch one day so they could be successful and make enough money. That is what Jesus gave them first when He met them. He gave them the biggest catch of their lifetime. It was a test—they passed that test and they left their boats, nets, and fish and followed Him (Luke 5:1–11). They walked away from it without having any attachment.

> So when they had brought their boats to land, they forsook all and followed Him. (Luke 5:11)

1. We Have to Die to the Desire to Become Rich

In our journeys to fulfilling God's kingdom assignment for us, the first thing we need to be free from is the desire to be rich. There is a stream of preachers who get stuck focusing on this stage. All they are focused on in their ministries and preaching is how to become wealthy. Many fall prey to this deception, and they will use any tactic or gimmick to make a little more money and fleece ignorant believers who are greedy for money.

> But those who desire to be rich fall into temptation and a snare, and *into* many foolish and harmful lusts which drown men in destruction and perdition. (1 Timothy 6:9)

Every individual dreams of having financial freedom. They start businesses and try all kinds of get-rich-quick schemes to be financially free. However, many end up in deep trouble, and some will even end up in prison or lose their lives as a result.

There is a legitimate way to become financially free and not have to worry about money. It comes by discovering your kingdom assignment. Your kingdom assignment package includes *everything* you need in your life to fulfill that assignment. That is the true freedom and financial security Jesus offers to every human being on this planet.

Once you begin to walk in your kingdom assignment, you don't need to worry about where the resources, money, or food are going to come from. It becomes God's responsibility to provide for you. That is why Jesus taught us to pray to the Father for our daily bread. It is His job to provide for us.

Many today follow Jesus for the "biggest catch" and the desire to be rich and successful. The sad thing is that many people talk about the kingdom and present it in such a way to teach people how to achieve their goals and dreams. But these people are not educated about the kingdom of God; they are agents of the Babylonian system. They are wolves in sheep's clothing.

If you come into the kingdom to become successful and rich, you are not going to have a fun ride. God will take you through the eye of a needle. You will be crying for your life because it will hurt every atom in your body to go through that process of entering the kingdom. Once you start walking in your kingdom assignment, it becomes the responsibility of the King and His kingdom to provide and protect you.

2. We Have to Die to the Desire to Be Great

The second ambition the disciples had to die to was their desire to be the greatest. This was the argument that they seemed to have the most. They argued about who was with Jesus when He did certain miracles and who did the most and the best to help Him do something. That is a step we have to go through in becoming a kingdom citizen—to die to that ambitious desire to become great leaders.

> Then a dispute arose among them as to which of them would be greatest. (Luke 9:46)

As ministers and believers, we will go through this stage. We will go through a season in our lives where we will run after positions and try to be the best and the greatest. We will look at some rich and famous people and wish in our hearts to be like them. Others will run after leadership and teachings about different leadership styles and tricks.

There is a simple way to feel great in the kingdom of God and in the body of Christ: Find your specific assignment, and then find where you fit in it, and start flowing in your gifts. That is the only thing that is required of each one of us. There is no need to learn any special charismatic gymnastics.

Jesus said of John the Baptist, "Assuredly, I say to you, among those born of women there has not risen one greater than John the Baptist; but he who is least in the kingdom of heaven is greater than he." (Matthew 11:11)

John the Baptist did not own a mansion, nor did he write any books of the Bible. Jesus called him the greatest among those born of women. Why? It is because of the unique assignment he fulfilled for the kingdom.

Each member of our body is essential to its overall function. When one part is missing or hurting, it affects the rest of the body. That is the way it is in the body of Christ. Nobody taught us how to function in the kingdom without betrayal and backbiting.

Many ministers get stuck at this stage. They are trying hard to be the greatest and the most famous of all time. They are all trying to build the largest church in their towns or cities and will organize campaigns and conferences to attract crowds. If we brought together a group of ministers, their internal struggle would be to know who is the greatest among them and who has the largest church or can draw the largest crowd.

3. We Have to Die to Wanting to Build Things for Jesus

The next ambition the disciples had to die to was trying or wishing to build something for Jesus. Remember when Jesus took Peter, James, and John to the Mount of Transfiguration? When they had that special experience with the Lord, Peter said he wanted to build three tabernacles: one for Jesus, one for Elijah, and a third for Moses.

It is normal for people to build a ministry and church, or even denominations, based on the experience of a leader they had in the past. They think they are building it for Jesus. Every denomination tells the story of its leader and how great and wonderful he or she was. The truth is that the people do not have anything to show in their lives now and they are living in the memory of something that happened to someone hundreds of years ago.

Do not build a ministry, monument, denomination, or an enterprise based on an experience you had with the Lord or on a gift. Do not follow someone who had one, either. Everything has to be built on Jesus and His kingdom. We need to keep moving to the next stage. These are all tests and different stages the Lord was taking them through.

There was a time in my life when I thought all I needed for ministry was a nice building for our church and the projects we were doing. Then when we had the building, we did not have any more projects to do. The building sat empty for more than eight years.

Then Jesus reminded me that He trained His twelve disciples without owning any buildings. These men turned out to be the most effective apostles that the kingdom and church has ever seen. That is what I learned during this pandemic—we have trained more people from around the world through technology than I did using our physical building or when I was traveling.

Everyone who is called by God has to go through these processes. Many do not complete the process; they stop somewhere along the way and build something for themselves using the name of Jesus and His kingdom based on a spiritual experience or vision they had.

We might think Peter's idea was noble because he wanted to build something for Jesus. I know many people killed themselves or lost their lives because they were working so hard trying to build something for Jesus. They think all the sacrifice they made for the sake of ministry was for Jesus, but He is not impressed with the sacrifices we make that He did not require.

If you visit Israel today, you will see monuments all throughout the land, and they are occupied and managed by various religious sects. They believe that they built those monuments for God or Jesus, but in reality, it became a source of income for many. God is not in any of them.

4. We Have to Die to the Desire for Position and Influence

The fourth ambition they had to die to was the desire to sit on the right and left side of Jesus—the ambition for position and influence. Remember, one of their mothers even came to Jesus requesting that her sons get that privilege. In the church world today, the fight is over who is closest to the apostle or the megachurch pastor.

> And He said to her, "What do you wish?" She said to Him, "Grant that these two sons of mine may sit, one on Your right hand and the other on the left, in Your kingdom." (Matthew 20:21)

There is so much jealousy and envy in church based on who is doing what. Everybody wants to feel significant. Many want positions so they can have control or to be seen by people. They want to feel important. The same principle I mentioned above applies here. Find your purpose and place in the kingdom, and you will feel significant.

5. We Have to Trust Jesus to Provide for Us

The fifth process they had to go through was moving from trusting in their own hands to provide for themselves to trusting Jesus and His kingdom for their provision. People will come up with all kinds of business ideas and money-generating scams to fleece the people.

Even Peter went back to fishing after Jesus was crucified. He thought that he had to do something to take care of himself and his family. I understand how Peter felt—when he had a child crying for food in his house, he felt compelled to do something.

> Simon Peter, Thomas called the Twin, Nathanael of Cana in Galilee, the sons of Zebedee, and two others of His disciples were together. Simon Peter said to them, "I am going fishing." They said to him, "We are going with you also." They went out and immediately got into the boat, and that night they caught nothing. (John 21:2–3)

Peter forgot that Jesus told them to seek His kingdom and His righteousness and then all the things they needed would be provided for them. It applies to us even today. Jesus and His kingdom never change; He is the same yesterday, today, and forever.

I have seen many ministers and believers who tried to start businesses to make money for the kingdom. They might say, "I am going to make enough money first to support myself, and then serve God with the rest of the time and money." I have not seen it work even once. Unless you are called to do this, it will not work for you. So many people promised me money through their business ventures that they were waiting to start. But nothing has come through yet. It has been more than twenty years.

Once you commit your life to fulfill what you are called to do in the kingdom, it is the King and the kingdom that are responsible to provide for you. You do not need to worry about where the provision is going to come from. It will take us a while to reach the place of learning to trust God and His kingdom for our provision. The earlier in life we start this, the easier it gets.

Peter could not catch anything that night, either. Jesus came with breakfast in the morning and gave it to them. Your provision is connected to your assignment in the kingdom.

6. We Have to Die to Getting Revenge

The sixth selfish ambition they had to die to was the tendency of taking revenge on their enemies or people who reject them. One day, a village in Samaria did not receive Jesus and His team. They rejected them and told them to leave their village. How did the disciples respond? They asked Jesus if they could bring fire from heaven and consume the whole village. Jesus' reply was that the Son of Man did not come to kill, but to save.

> And when His disciples James and John saw *this,* they said, "Lord, do You want us to command fire to come down from heaven and consume them, just as Elijah did?" But He turned and rebuked them, and said, "You do not know what manner of spirit you are of. For the Son of Man did not come to destroy men's lives but to save *them.*" (Luke 9:54–56)

There are many today who cry out for fire on their enemies or on the people who hate them or do not receive them. Jesus said that this mentality is not from His Spirit, but from the spirit that works in the Gentiles. Many of their prayers are about praying fire on their enemies. If you wish your enemies were dead, then you are not ready for Jesus and His kingdom yet. We are lording it over people like the leaders of this world system.

We are supposed to bless our enemies and pray for those who curse or persecute us. That is what Jesus told us to do. He told us to rejoice when people say evil things about us and despitefully use us because our reward is great in heaven (Matthew 5:11–12).

7. We Have to Die to Thinking Our Way Is Right

The next ambition the disciples had to die to was feeling they were the only ones who were doing things right or authorized to do ministry. Many believe they received the best and the most important revelation and everyone should listen to them or come under their umbrella.

When the disciples saw that others were doing ministry, casting out demons, and baptizing more people, they became jealous. They wanted Jesus to go and tell those other people to stop it or join them. They thought they were the only ones who had the license from Jesus to preach the kingdom and do ministry.

> Now John answered Him, saying, "Teacher, we saw someone who does not follow us casting out demons in Your name, and we forbade him because he does not follow us." (Mark 9:38)

There are leaders and ministers today who feel the same way. They think they are the only true ministers and everybody else is a second-class citizen. Because they belong to some particular race or nationality or denomination, they feel they received the "wholesale business rights" from heaven and everybody else must buy it from them for a retail price, or become their franchisee. That self-centered, evil ambition must die!

Every denomination thinks they are the best and that they have it all together. But the truth is that they have only received a piece of the puzzle, not the whole thing. When we bring all the pieces together, that is when we see the big picture. It is the same with different ministries; they run with what they have, thinking that is all people need. They carry just one aspect of the truth, not the whole truth.

We need to appreciate and receive what each believer, minister, ministry, and denomination brings to the table. If we do not, we will have a skewed perspective of God and His kingdom.

8. We Have to Die to Wanting to Get Something Out of It

The eighth ambition they needed to die to was thinking, *"What's in it for me?"* Remember when Peter asked Jesus, "We've given up everything to follow you. What will we get?" (Matthew 19:27, NLT). No matter what we do, at some point in life this same question will arise in our hearts.

What's in it for me? We need to overcome this stage when it comes to following Jesus in our marriage, work, ministry, or politics. We follow His footsteps. What was in it for Him when He came down to this cursed planet to live as a human? He did that for us. Then He said there is no greater love than someone laying down his life for his friends (John 15:13).

We are not serving God for what we can get out of Him. That is the most selfish motive to do anything. Whether in marriage, work, or business, when this thought arises in people's hearts, they become self-seeking and will not be faithful in their service to God.

9. We Have to Die to Self-Preservation

The next ambition they had to die to was loving their own lives, or self-preservation. Remember the night before Jesus was crucified? Most of the disciples ran for their lives, and Peter denied Him three times. If we run in the face of a challenge, trying to protect ourselves, then we are not living in His kingdom. Self-preservation and loving our own lives are dangerous in the kingdom. Jesus said if we try to save our lives, we will lose them, but if we lose our lives for the sake of Jesus and His kingdom, we will save them. (Mark 8:35)

> Then all the disciples forsook Him and fled.
> (Matthew 26:56b)

These disciples forgot all the promises Jesus told them. He promised them that He would never leave them. He said that not even one hair would fall from their heads without Him knowing. He told them countless times not to be afraid and gave many other great promises. But in the midst of their challenge, those promises did not mean anything to them. Their motto was to protect and save themselves at any cost.

10. We Have to Die to Nationalism

The last ambition they had to die to was nationalism. The disciples' last question to Jesus just before He ascended to heaven was to ask if He was now going to establish a kingdom for Israel (Acts 1:6). After all that training and teaching, they could not understand the scope of God's kingdom—even though Jesus was sent to the lost sheep of Israel, because the Messiah was promised to them. But His kingdom was not just meant for Israel.

> Therefore, when they had come together, they asked Him, saying, "Lord, will You at this time restore the kingdom to Israel?" (Acts 1:6)

They didn't even remember the kingdom prayer He taught them which said that He wants His kingdom to come to the whole earth, not just in Israel or in Jerusalem. Jesus said the gospel of the kingdom needs to be preached in all the world and in every nation as a witness (Matthew 24:14).

Jesus' reply to them was to go to the ends of the earth. He wanted them to cross every cultural, racial, language, religious, and tribalistic boundary. His kingdom is for the entire earth—for every nation and for all people.

That is the reason the Jewish leaders asked to free Barabbas. He was a political leader who promised the restoration of their national pride. He even attempted a revolt against Rome and ended up in prison. He promised freedom from the oppression of Rome. When people are desperate for their survival, they will throw away their sense of ethics and truth and align with anyone.

We need to be careful about who we are marching behind and aligning ourselves with politically. Make sure it is not a Barabbas. We have only one King, and His name is Jesus Christ. There is only one kingdom, and that is the kingdom of our Lord and Christ. Do not fall for the nationalistic spirit that is moving through the nations. It is a counterfeit to the kingdom movement.

Unfortunately, many believers think the same today. They think the kingdom of God is in Israel or in Jerusalem. But Jesus said that He wants this kingdom message to be taken to the ends of the earth. The kingdom of God is for the whole earth and for all people from every nation (Matthew 8:11).

PROGRESSING THROUGH THE STAGES

If you examine the body of Christ today, you will find out there are various streams of ministries and belief systems that are stuck in any one of these stages. There are ministers who pray and speak vengeance upon their enemies like the disciples wanted to do. Every time they are praying fire on their enemies, they are stuck in that stage.

Every single believer and minister are somewhere along these ten stages of training mentioned above. You can examine your life and decide which stage you are in. Keep moving and do not get stuck in any one of them.

It is absolutely fine to change streams. You need to keep moving until you reach a place in your heart where you are willing to lay down your life for the King and His kingdom. Just like people lay down their lives for their countries by joining the army, we need people who are sold out for the kingdom. God can only use these people to build His kingdom, and until each one of us reaches that stage, we will be building our own kingdoms, businesses, or ministries using the name of Jesus.

In the olden days, citizens died for their king and his kingdom while fighting enemies in battles. They died for their earthly king and kingdom. Even today, soldiers die fighting for their countries. The disciples reached that stage by God's grace and by the power of the Holy Spirit. Remember, because of fear, these same disciples ran for their lives once, but later they died for Him.

As you go through these stages, do not feel condemned in your heart because you "camped" longer than you should have at one of these stages. Pick up the tent and keep moving because you have a job to do in the kingdom. The King needs you!

When the early disciples passed all these stages, they were willing to die for their King and His kingdom. History shows that they all died as martyrs except John. We need to reach the place Adam was before the fall and where Jesus was when He came to the earth. They were here to do the will of their Father. Adam had no selfish ambition or desire to be successful or to build anything for himself. His assignment was given to Him by his Father. Jesus said the same thing: "I came to do the will of Him who sent me" (John 6:38).

Only when someone passes all the stages can God trust him or her with the resources and treasures of His kingdom. That is when He releases us to disciple nations. Until then, we are either in the training process, under the Egyptian religious system, or blinded by the Babylonian entertainment system.

When we are able to truly say we are ready to die for our King and His kingdom from our hearts, then we are ready to live the kingdom life and manifest it on the earth. Then we are ready to manifest the kingdom and the glory of God to the rest of creation. Dying to self and to our ambitions is a daily walk. Desiring to be successful and to become a great leader will try to creep into our hearts at any moment. That is why it is so important to guard our hearts and minds.

It is not easy for us to die to ourselves, especially for those of us who grew up in Western culture hearing about the American dream all of our lives. So God has to take us through the eye of the needle and when we come out on the other side, we will not be the same people or in the same shape as when we started the journey!

When the disciples heard Jesus talk this way, they said, "Lord, this is tough. Who can be saved then?" (see Matthew 19:25). Jesus' response was to say that the way to life is narrow and not many will find it, but the way to destruction is broad and many travel that path.

> Because narrow *is* the gate and difficult *is* the way which leads to life, and there are few who find it. (Matthew 7:14)

> Strive to enter through the narrow gate, for many, I say to you, will seek to enter and will not be able. (Luke 13:24)

May the Lord help each one of us find that way to life. We have lived enough days for ourselves trying to be successful and chasing various dreams. One thing about life is that when we get what we thought we wanted, we realize that was not the thing we actually wanted. Sometimes we reach a place or position in life and we realize that it wasn't the place or position we really wanted. This journey will continue until we discover the kingdom of God and His assignment for us.

This does not mean you can't do business or become a political leader. You have to do what you are called to do for the right reason. Kingdom is all about sonship. The nutshell of life in the kingdom is becoming a son of the King in His kingdom to do His will. We are here to do the will of our Father who sent us to this planet, just like Jesus was. When we are empty of ourselves, dead to all ambitions and wants, and God can freely flow through us, then we are ready to live the lives God wants us to live. Welcome to the kingdom life!

I had to go through this process in my life. My goal in life is not to build a big ministry or to make a name for myself. I already went through that stage. I have given my life over to the Lord; I eat, breathe, and dream about being with Him to see His kingdom established in people's lives first, and then in the nations.

CHAPTER 16

THREE KINDS OF PEOPLE WE NEED TO FULFILL OUR KINGDOM ASSIGNMENT

It is impossible to fulfill our God-given assignment on our own. Everything in the kingdom flows through relationships. We need all kinds of people on our way to fulfilling our destiny. There are some key people we cannot avoid, and we need to be careful how we treat them and how we react when God allows them to come to us and do what they were sent to do.

Many of us think we just need to be connected with some millionaires to fulfill what God has called us to do. We do need people with different resources, but this chapter is not about those people. This is about a particular kind of people, and without them, we will not fulfill our kingdom assignment.

We Need Judases

When Jesus selected His twelve disciples, they were people with different personalities and gifts. Every one of them was essential in fulfilling His assignment—including Judas, who betrayed Him. That is the first kind of person we "need" to fulfill our kingdom assignment—Judases. To fulfill our calling, we need not only people like Peter, James, and John, but people like Judas.

Peter, James, and John are willing to give their lives for you, but Judas doesn't care about your life or your mission. This is the main difference between these two groups. Judases are there for themselves; they do not care what happens to you, what you go through, or what they will put you through, as long as they get what they want.

On our way to fulfilling our destiny, we will encounter some Judases in our lives. These will be the people we trained and in whom we invested our time and resources, but at the end, they will turn against us and betray us.

The pain they will cause will be unbearable and you will be shocked, wondering how it could happen and how a human being could do such things. Have you experienced any such incidents in your life yet? If not, get ready; they will come.

Without Judas, Jesus would not have fulfilled His assignment. Imagine if Jesus didn't go to the cross. What would have happened to Him and the human race? It's unimaginable, right? Jesus purposefully selected Judas and trained him up. He knew what Judas would do to Him after three years. Knowing that, He still loved him and took care of him, because He needed him as much as He did the rest of the disciples.

Humanly speaking, it is impossible and unbearable to go through the pain Judases will cause in our lives. Only by the grace and help of the Holy Spirit can we forgive and move on. When we are moments away from our greatest breakthroughs in the kingdom, Judas will manifest and they will be the catalyst to propel us to the next level or to create the circumstances that will usher in what God has for us next.

We need to be careful how we treat our Judases. If we become bitter, angry, and offended, we will delay our promotion in the Spirit. We will have to go through the process again until the next Judas comes in the next season of life. Why should we go through the same pain more than once? It's not worth it, and it is very costly. It will cause an emotional toll on our health. Once we encounter the betrayal of a Judas, our lives will not be the same. That incident will cause a permanent shift or change in our personalities, mindsets, and worldviews.

Jesus would not have reached the cross without Judas. What if He had died by some other means and didn't go to the cross? The result would not be the same. Can you look back and see if you have ever encountered a Judas in your life? How did you handle them and the situation? Do you still harbor bitterness and unforgiveness in your heart, or did you forgive and let it go?

Many people carry their pain with them for the rest of their lives and never forgive their Judases. Why? It is because Judas wasn't a stranger; he or she was someone who was very close to them and in whom they put their trust. These are people who once said they would even die for you and would be your best friend forever, no matter what happened.

Now the question is: What prompted Judas to betray his Master? What was going in Judas' heart? What motivated him to take such a tragic step? It was self-preservation. He thought that if he did not take care of himself, his needs would not be met. Maybe he had financial need in his personal life or family, or he just had a desire to be rich.

Another reason Judas betrayed Jesus was because of greed and covetousness. As the Bible says, the love of money is the root of all evil. He was the treasurer of Jesus' ministry. He used to steal from the money bag. He thought he would be a little richer by receiving thirty more pieces of silver.

Jesus and His mission were not Judas' priority. Instead, his focus was on money and how much he could make. When people come to you to work with you, if their first question has to do with how much you are going to pay them, they will not last long. You cannot build anything with such people. Watch for the people who come to you because of the vision God gave you. They are God-sent and will be with you through thick and thin because their passion is the vision, not money.

There will not be very many who come because they are attracted to your vision. Pray that God will send them to you, or that He will send you to people because of the vision. Those who come because of money will betray you in the end, or they will do something unethical to get more money from you.

Remember that Judas was walking with the Creator of the universe. Jesus could have met any need he had in a moment of time if he had expressed it to Him. But Judas decided to take his life into his own hands and do the unthinkable. He was afraid and thought the only way to meet that need was to betray his Lord.

When people betray us, they do it to preserve themselves. They do not trust God and they allow their weaknesses to take over them. They feel legitimate and justified in what they do. The wound they inflict in us will be so deep that it will require supernatural grace to forgive and then be healed.

You cannot avoid Judases, and you cannot run away from them. They are essential to the process, and without them you will not reach your full potential. If you try to run away from Judases, you will sabotage God's plan for your life. The reason you are reading this is because God is trying to help you prepare for when this happens.

We Need King Sauls

The second kind of person you will need to fulfill your kingdom assignment is people like King Saul. The challenges David encountered on his way to fulfilling his purpose were not minor. After the victory over Goliath, David was brought to the palace to play music so that Saul might find some relief from his demonic oppression.

While David was in the palace, Saul was not happy with him. David did something Saul only dreamed of doing, or tried to do but couldn't: he killed the giant. That is the number one reason the Sauls in your life will become jealous of you. People who are jealous of what you do, what you carry, and the mantle that is upon you are Sauls in your life.

Saul was the king; he was supposed to be a father figure, encouraging and building up people like David for the future of the nation. But if the father figure is insecure, jealous, and immature, they will not train up and promote anyone else. They are afraid of losing their positions.

In the real situation, Saul should have been happy because he had a friend or servant like David. But he did not know how to manage David, so he considered him a threat instead of a blessing. That is what insecurity will do to us. We will end up fighting people who were sent by God to help us and become jealous of them. We will wish that they would disappear or even die, like when Saul tried many times to kill David.

Do not expect people who are over you to come and celebrate your anointing and your calling. It will not happen most of the time. I have spent many years looking for the approval of people who were above me. I thought if they would just recognize the revelation and the call of God on my life, I would be on my way to success. But that did not happen. Most of the time, it won't happen. Do not be discouraged if this happens to you.

Sauls are sent by God to teach us patience and longsuffering and how to love our enemies. David could have easily killed Saul, but David trusted God with his problem and did not take it into his own hands. That is the way we should be treating our Sauls. If we hate them and try to pay back in the flesh for what they have done to us, we will short-circuit the process and our destiny.

Believe it or not, there are people who are so jealous of you they cannot stand what you carry in the spirit. The anointing you carry irritates the demons in them. They hate you and would like to see you dead, but they will not be able to do you any harm. God will not let them harm you in any way if you keep your heart pure before Him. Do not react in the flesh to them and become like them.

Hand them over to the Lord and let Him take care of them. When the right time comes, He will do it. He will not remove them from your life as soon as you ask Him. The Sauls have been sent by God to accomplish a specific change in your heart toward life and toward people.

That is your final test before God launches you to fulfill your destiny. People who you think should help you, promote you, and encourage you will be the ones who turn against you and want to destroy you because of misunderstanding, insecurity, and control.

Saul was the one meant to encourage David and make room for his anointing in the kingdom. Instead, he thought David was a threat to his throne. People who are shortsighted will fight those who carry the seed of God.

The reason Saul told David to use his own armor was not because he was concerned about David's safety. If it were so, Saul would have given him a new armor; I'm sure there was a spare set around. I believe Saul's intent was that if David won against the giant, he could say it was because David had used his armor, that way, he could get the credit.

The reason some folks force you to do things the way they do or compel you to adopt their calling is because they want the credit. They don't want you to do anything different than what they are doing; they want you to be a copy of them. They do not believe in your identity or unique calling. They just want you to serve them and *their* calling.

We Need Joseph's Brothers

The third person or people you need to fulfill your kingdom assignment are Joseph's brothers. Joseph had eleven brothers, ten of whom could not stand him because he was different from them. He shared his dream with them, and they were not happy to hear it. They hated and rejected him.

As a result, they plotted to kill him, but because one of his brothers pleaded for his life, they decided to spare him and sell him as a slave instead. That was part of the plan and the process God had for Joseph. When you receive a dream from God and set out to fulfill your kingdom assignment, your own kith and kin and people from your own church will begin to reject you and the vision God gave you.

The moment you present your dream, you will begin to face unusual problems from people. It shows that God has started the process of fulfilling your dream. His ways are not our ways. Please know that nothing will happen in your life without His knowledge.

People you would have expected to celebrate you and your vision will turn against you and begin to persecute you. It happens this way all the time. You are not a stranger, and your case is not anything unusual. You will feel like nobody else has had to face what you have faced, but that is a lie from the enemy.

People who do not have a dream will hate those who have one. The reason Joseph's brothers rejected him was because they did not have dreams for their futures. Their outlooks on life were limited only to their immediate circumstances. They could not see anything beyond what their natural eyes could see.

But if they did not reject Joseph and sell him as a slave, he would not have reached Egypt. What would have happened if he had not reached Egypt? That was the only way he could have reached Egypt. His father was not going to send him to Egypt for higher studies or to do business if he wanted to go there.

God knows how to take us to the place where He wants us to be. He will use any means to do that. Most of the time it will be very painful;

other times, that pain is part of the process we need to go through in order to fulfill what He called us to do.

Wherever you are in life right now is not an accident. You can get bitter about it, or you can bring something better out of the situation, like Joseph did. Wherever he went, he brought the best out of the situations and the people around him.

On your way to fulfilling your kingdom assignment, you will encounter some people who will reject you and your vision. Do not expect everyone to open their arms and embrace you and accept what you carry. Both people who accept and reject you are essential to you in fulfilling your calling. You cannot do it without them!

Don't let bitterness spring up in your heart toward those who reject you. Our natural reaction is to become upset and pay them back for what they have done. But if you do, you will not reach the place of your destiny. Let God handle it for you.

Those are the three kinds of people you will need and will encounter in your journey of fulfilling your kingdom assignment. When you encounter them, now you will know what to do and how to deal with them. May the Lord give you the wisdom to do so.

I believe you have been blessed, challenged, and transformed by reading this book. This is not my book; it was given to me by the Holy Spirit. I strongly recommend you read it a couple of times and really study it. Join the online course called God's Original Design: *Kingdom Secrets to Financial Provision and Security*, by registering for it on our website: www.TheKingdomNetwork.org/School. Thank you so much and God bless you.

MORE BOOKS & RESOURCES

DISCIPLING NATIONS SERIES

Kingdom Mandate (for any donation)
Discovering the Lost Kingdom (Volume 1) $14.00
Purpose, Calling, and Gifts (Volume 2) $15.00
God's Original Design (Volume 3) $20.00
Seeing, Entering, and Manifesting the Kingdom of God (Volume 4)$20.00
The Ekklesia (Volume 5) $30.00
The Gospel of the Kingdom (Volume 6) $20.00
Power and Authority of the Church (Volume 7) $15.00
Kingdom Family (Volume 8) $15.00
The Birthing of a kingdom nation (Volume 9) $20.00
What happened to God (Volume10) $20.00
7 Dimensions and Operations of the Kingdom of God (Volume 11)$15.00
Kingdom Economy (Volume 12) $15.00
Kingdom Government (Volume 13) $15.00
Releasing Kings and Queens to their Original Intent (Volume 14) $10.00
Kingdom Secrets to Restoring Nations Back to God (Volume 15) $20.00

KINGDOM LIVING SERIES

The Three Most Important Decisions of Your Life $15.00
Keys to Passing Your Spiritual Tests $15.00
Recognizing God's Timing for Your Life $12.00
Overcoming the Spirit of Poverty $10.00
Seven Kinds of Believers $10.00
7 Dimensions of God's Glory $5.00
7 Dimensions of God's Grace $10.00
7 Kinds of Faith $7.00

KINGDOM BOOKS FOR KIDS

Genesis 126 Three Volume Book set for boys $25.00

TO PLACE AN ORDER:

www.TheKingdomNetwork.org
Phone: 1-800-558-5020
Email: info@TheKingdomNetwork.org

Are you struggling to discover your **PURPOSE ?**
You are not supposed to fit in but stand out !

Sign up today for the upcoming
FREE Online Kingdom Course

DISCOVERING
THE LOST KINGDOM

In this course you'll DISCOVER:

>> Your true identity and purpose
>> What God is doing on the earth and how you can partner with Him in it
>> Why God created the earth and put us on this planet
   And much more ...

Why are people becoming more and more disinterested in **church and religion** globally?
Join the course, and discover
what your soul has been searching for all along.

FREE BOOK AND STUDY GUIDE

other courses available
>> DISCOVERING PURPOSE, CALLING AND GIFTS
>> SEEING, ENTERING AND MANIFESTING THE KINGDOM
>> GOD'S ORIGINAL DESIGN | FEBRUARY 2024
>> The Ekklesia
>> The Next move of GOD
   And more ...

Register Now @ **www.TheKingdomUniversity.org**

www.ingramcontent.com/pod-product-compliance
Lightning Source LLC
Chambersburg PA
CBHW070051080526
44586CB00013B/1009